Sabine Moritz

ROSES

Sabine Moritz

ROSES

37 Drawings

HENI PUBLISHING
LONDON 2010

The Green Windbreaker

When my father strolled through Paris,
often in the green windbreaker
that he had ordered tailor-made
(one of the few luxuries
in his rather modest life),
when he spent long hours in the Louvre,
studying the paintings of Corot and the other minor
masters from centuries past,
I still didn't know, I couldn't know,
how much destruction still lay hidden
in the years just then approaching,
as if that green windbreaker
had brought him ill luck,
but now I begin to recognize,
to suspect that catastrophe
had been stitched into all his clothing,
regardless of size or shape,
and even the greatest master-painters
could offer no assistance here.

— Adam Zagajewski, 2009

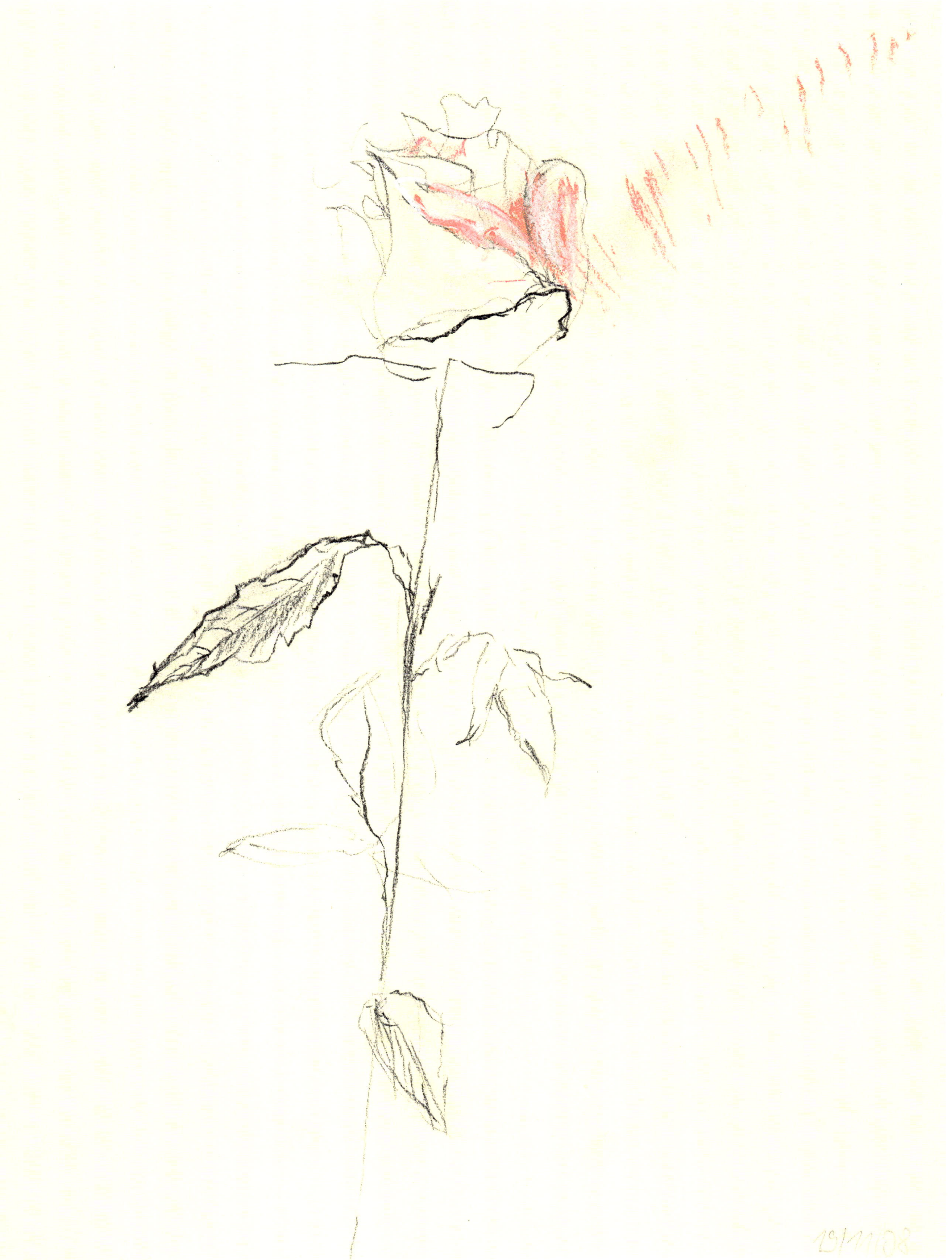

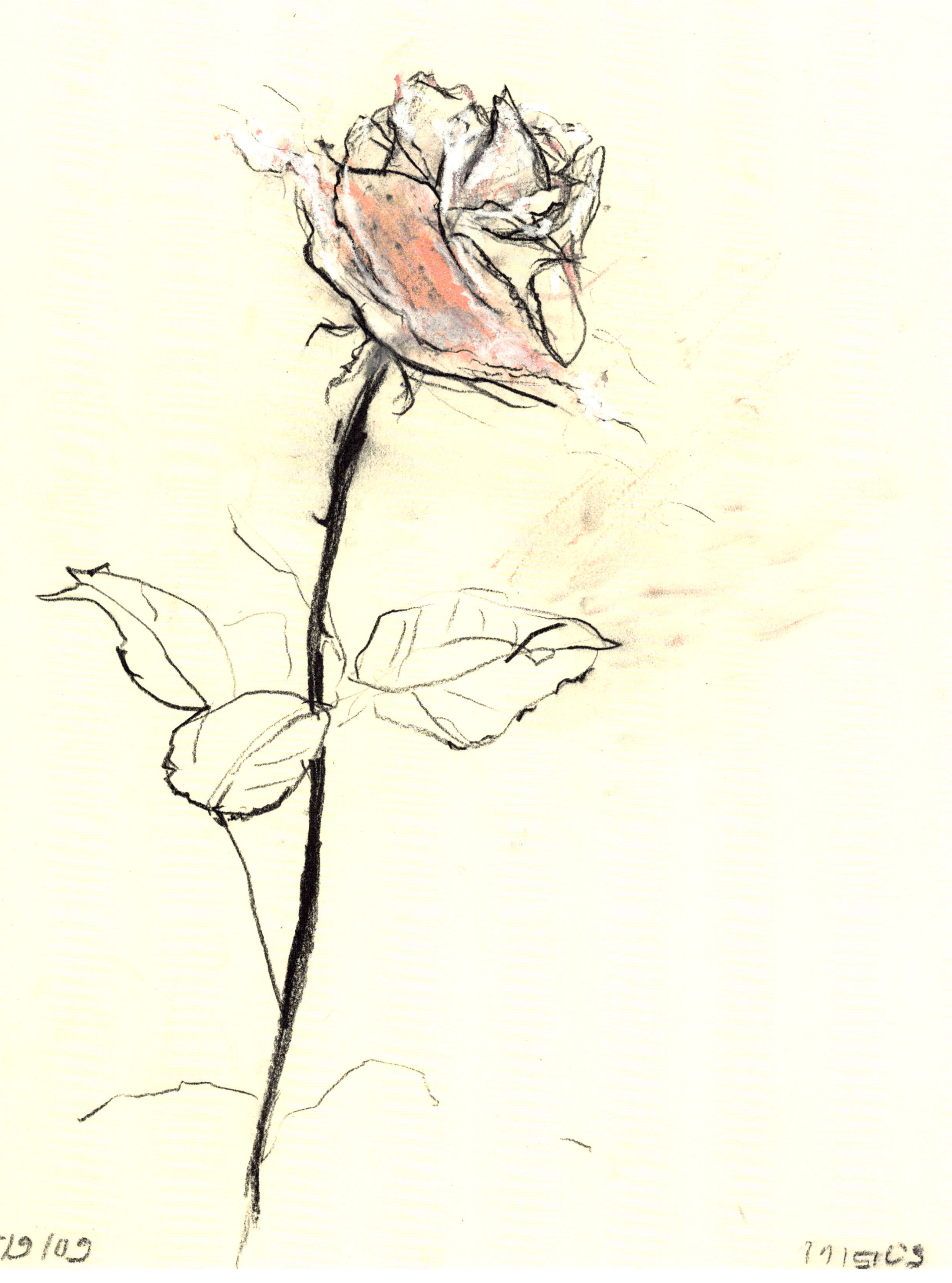
5|9|09
11|5|09

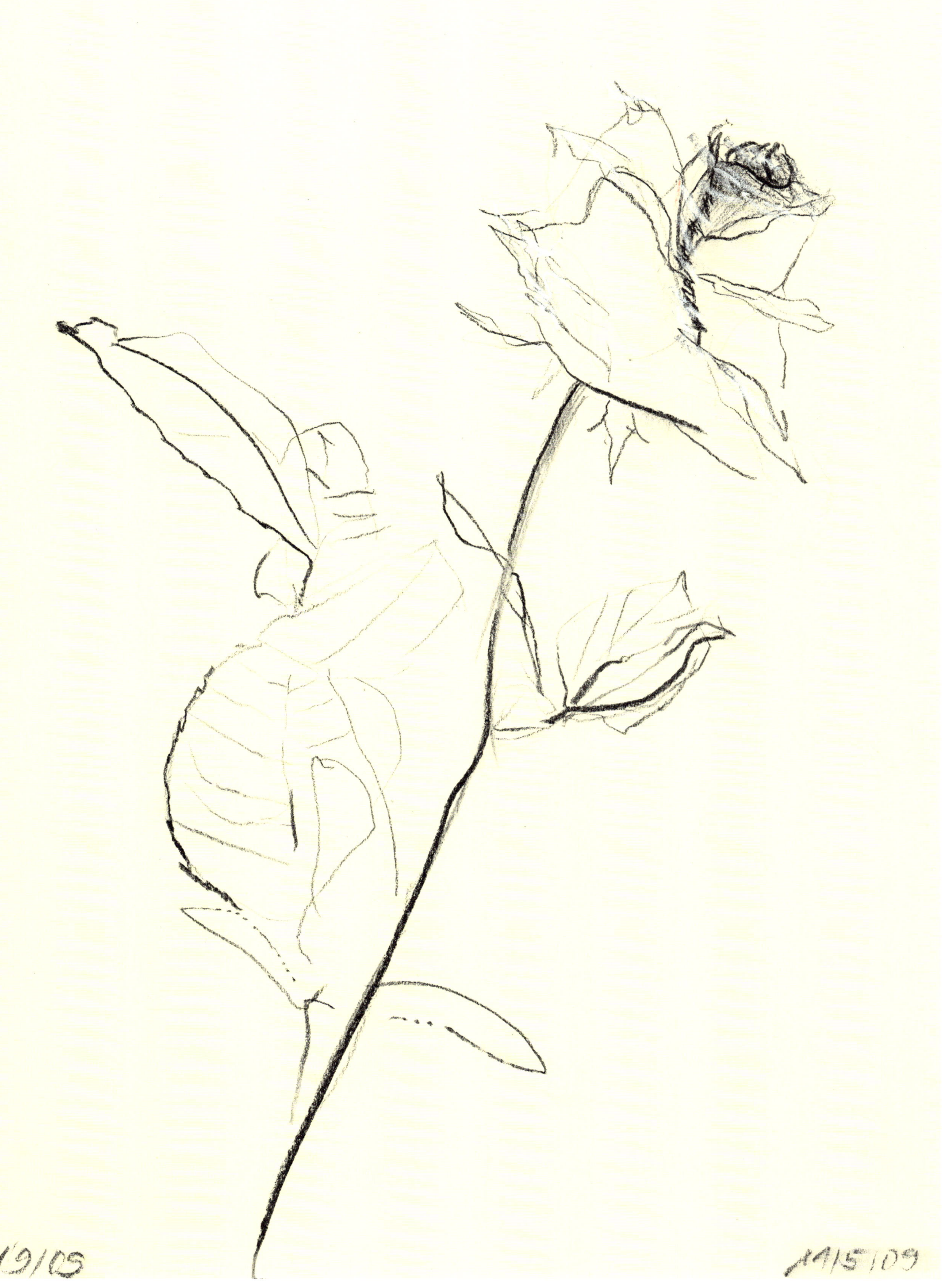

5/9/05
11/5/09

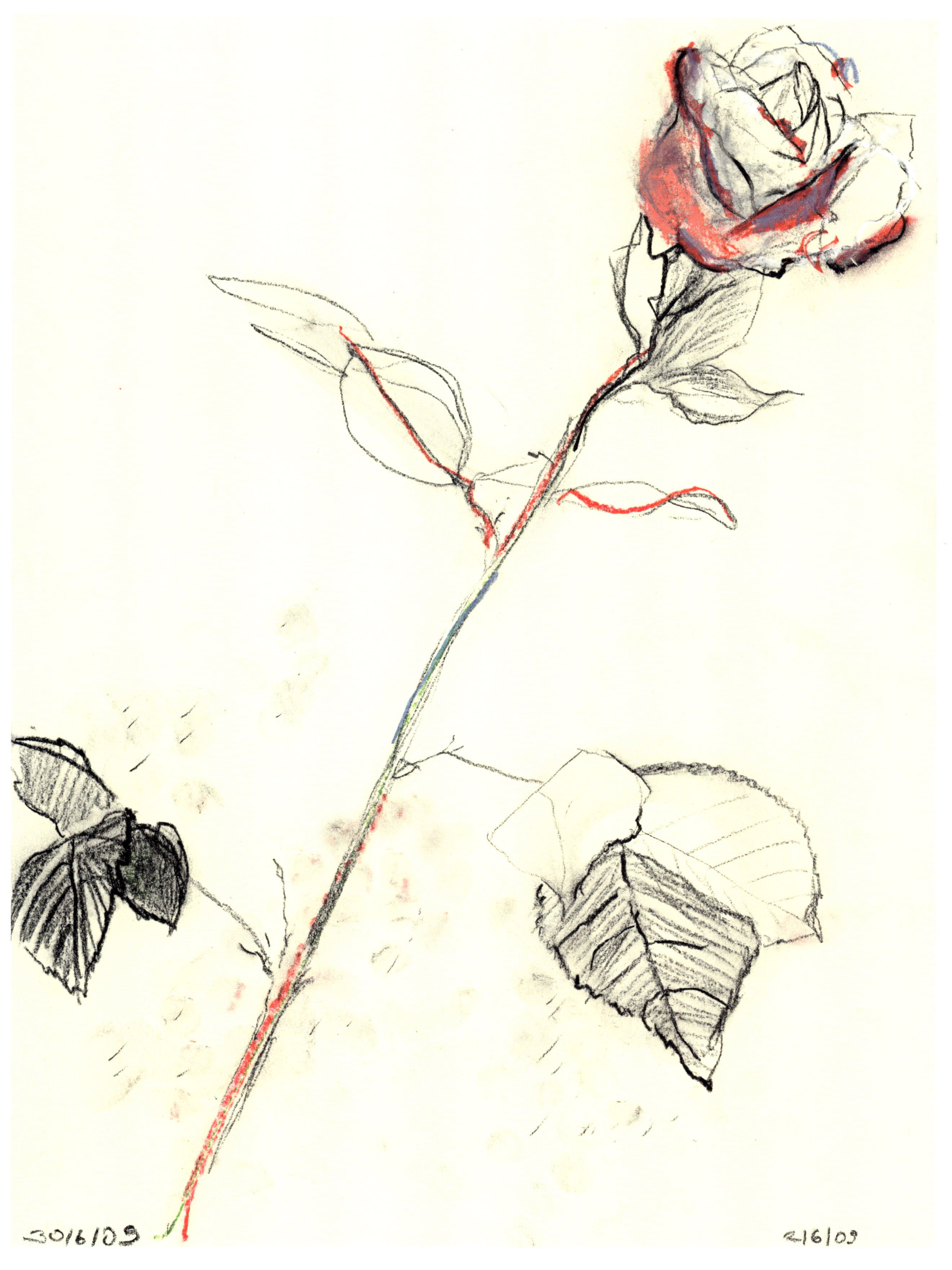

30/6/09
2/6/09

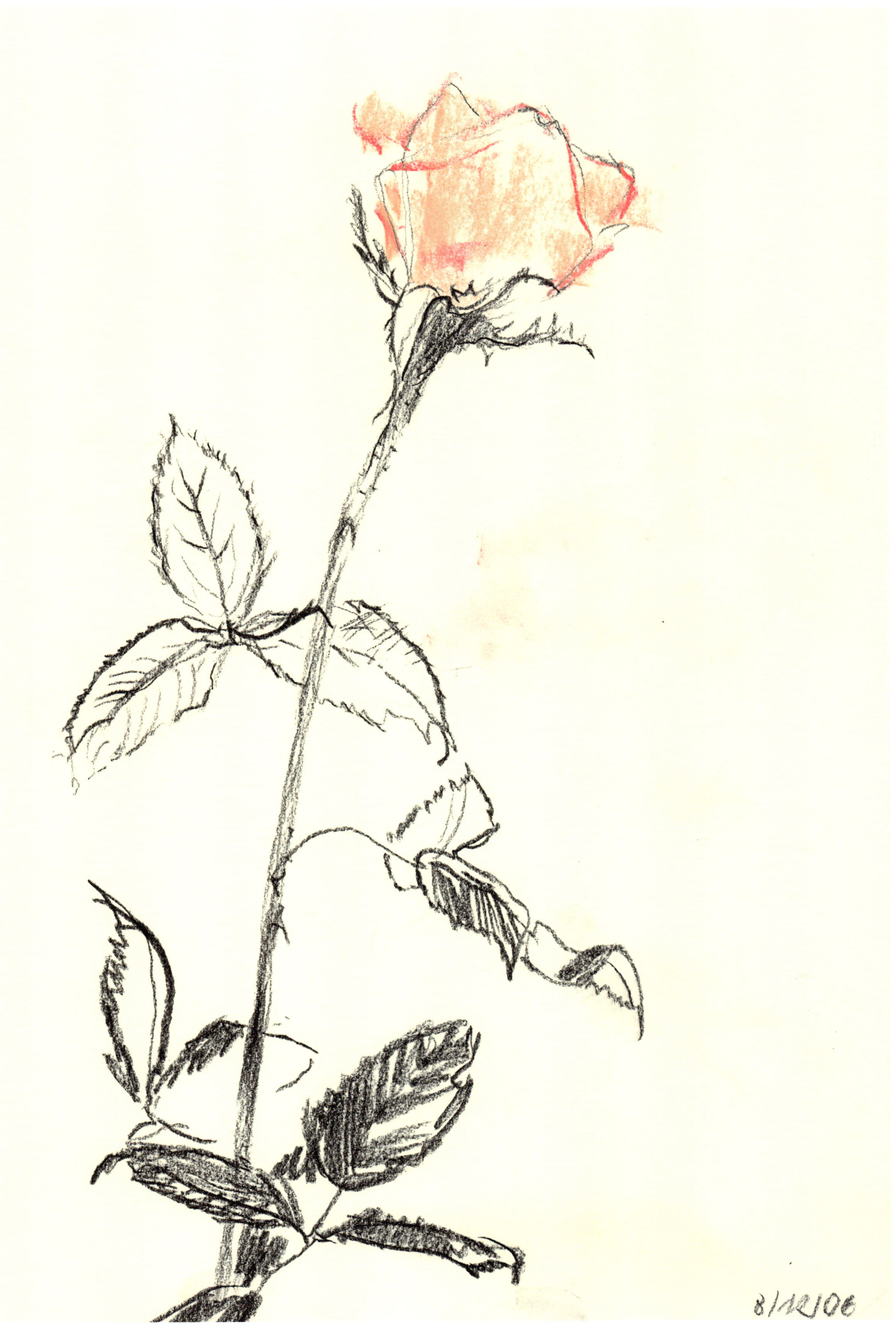

8/12/06

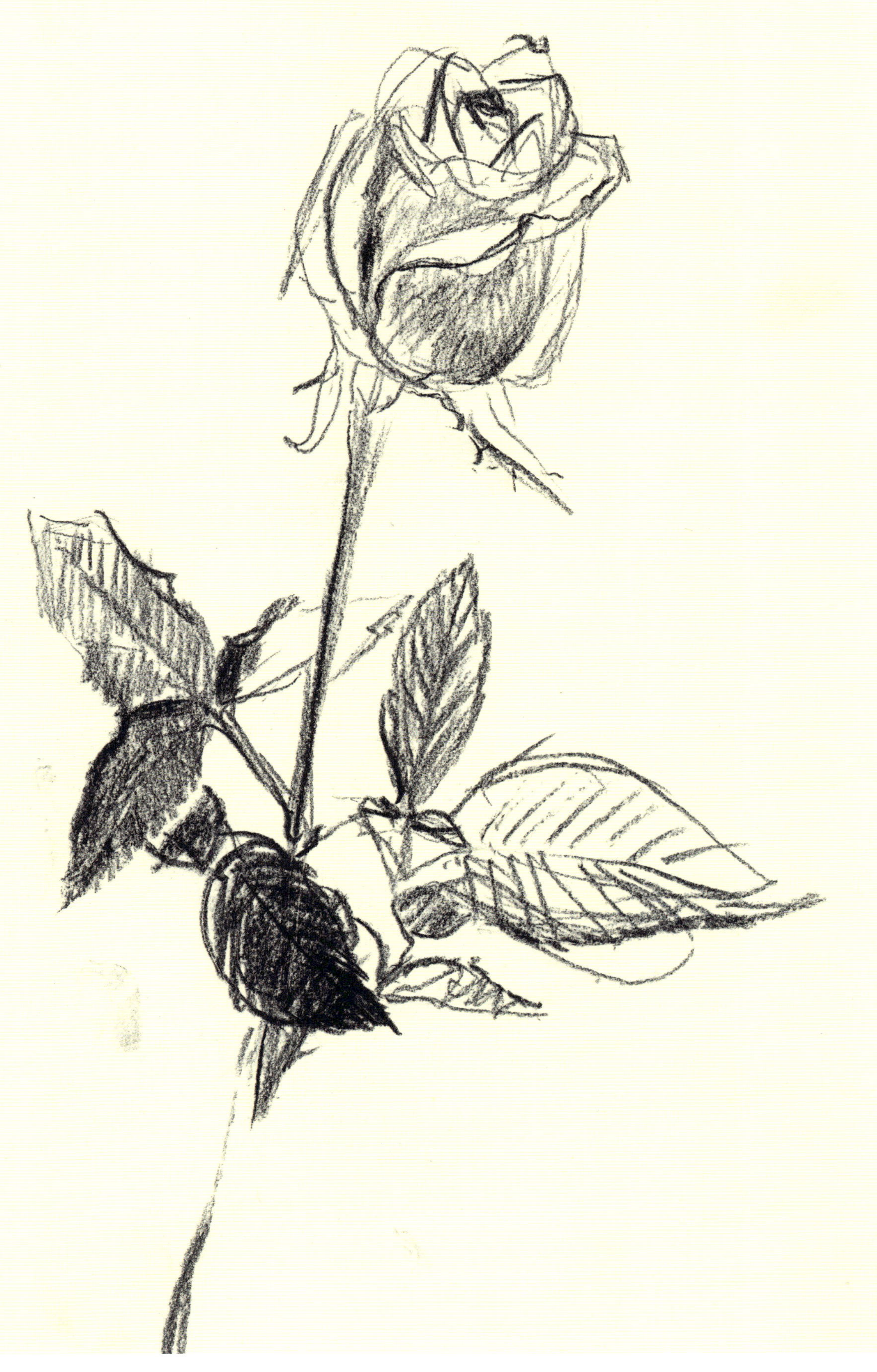

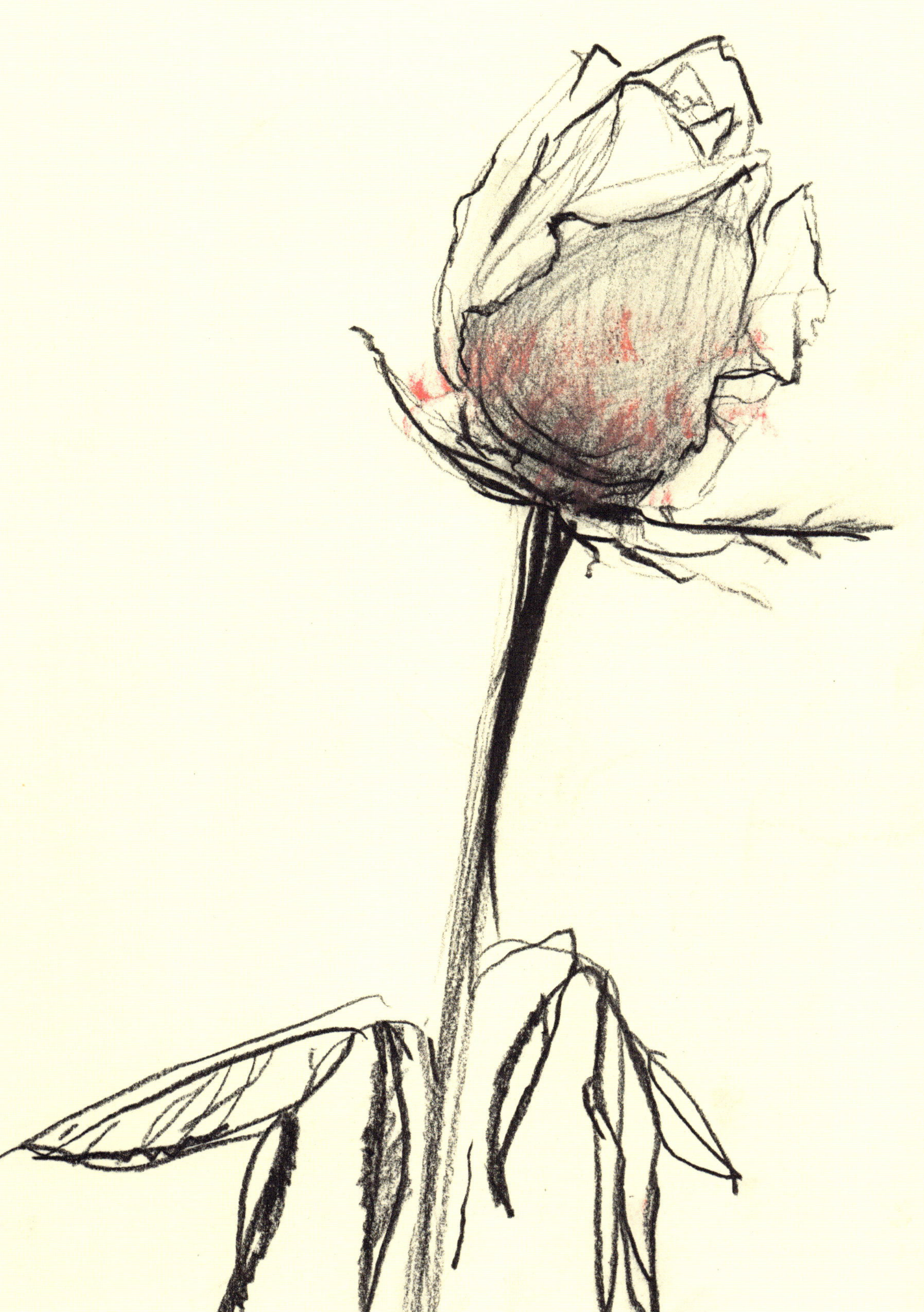

6/12/06

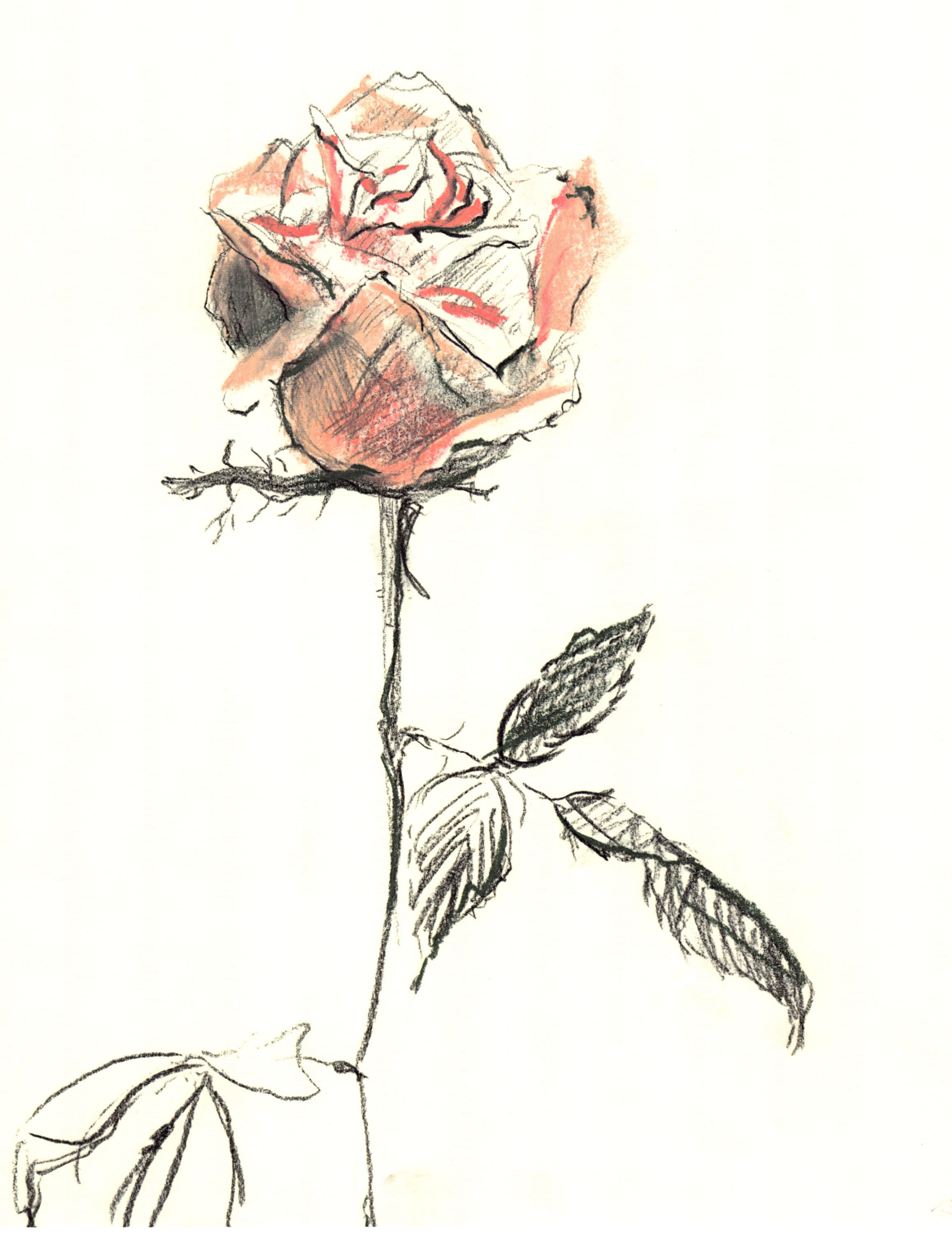

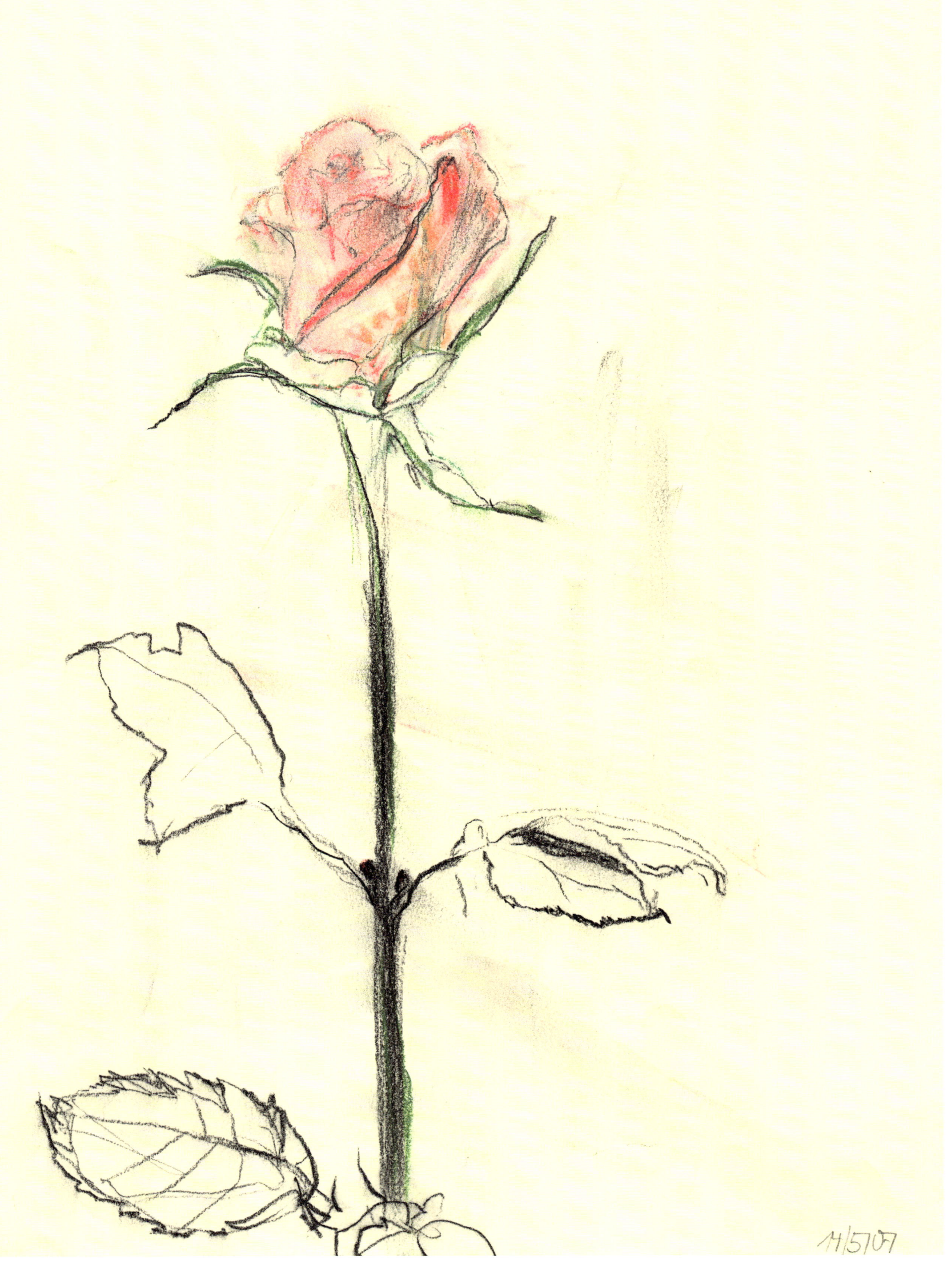

11/5/07

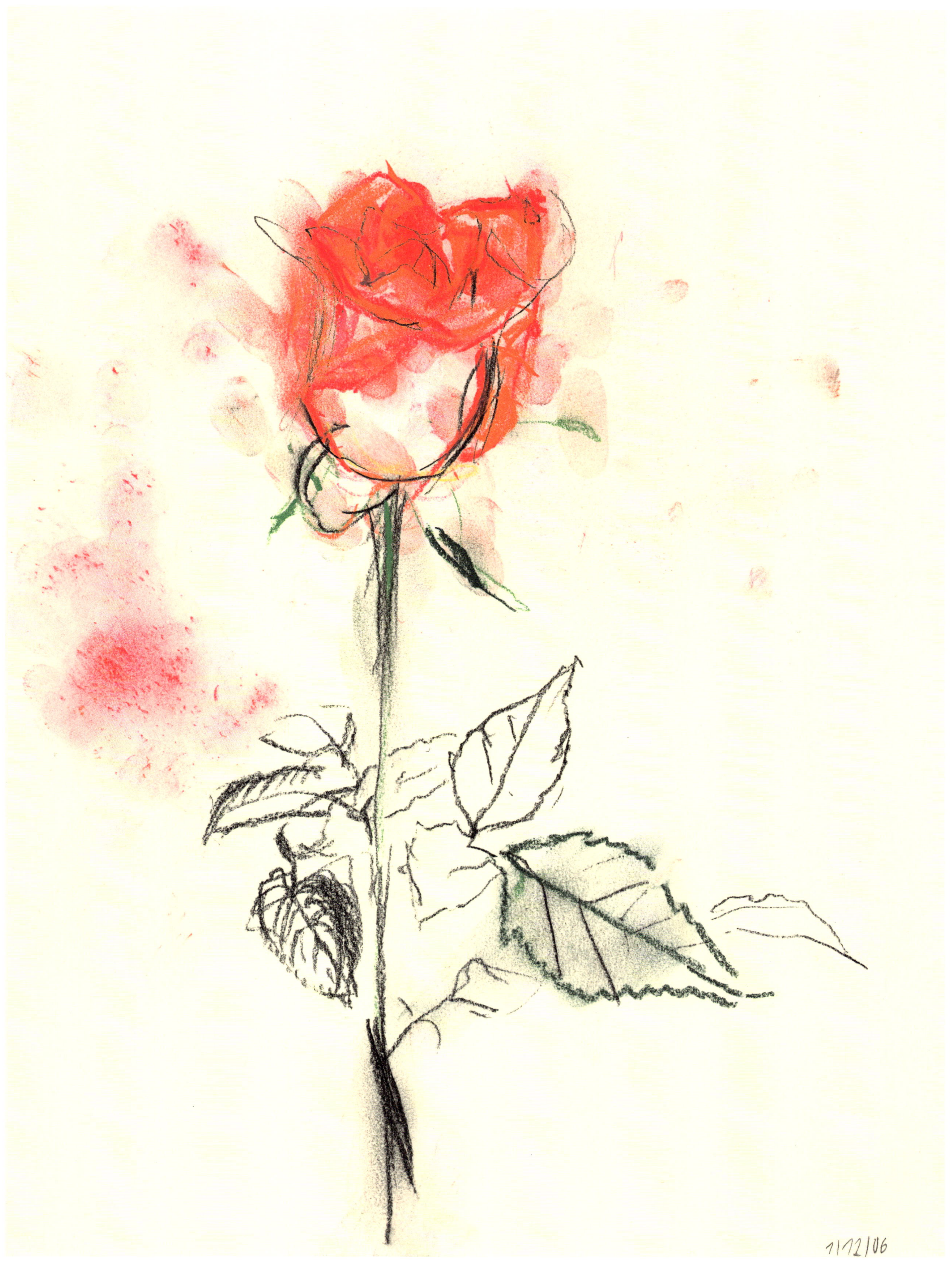

1/12/06

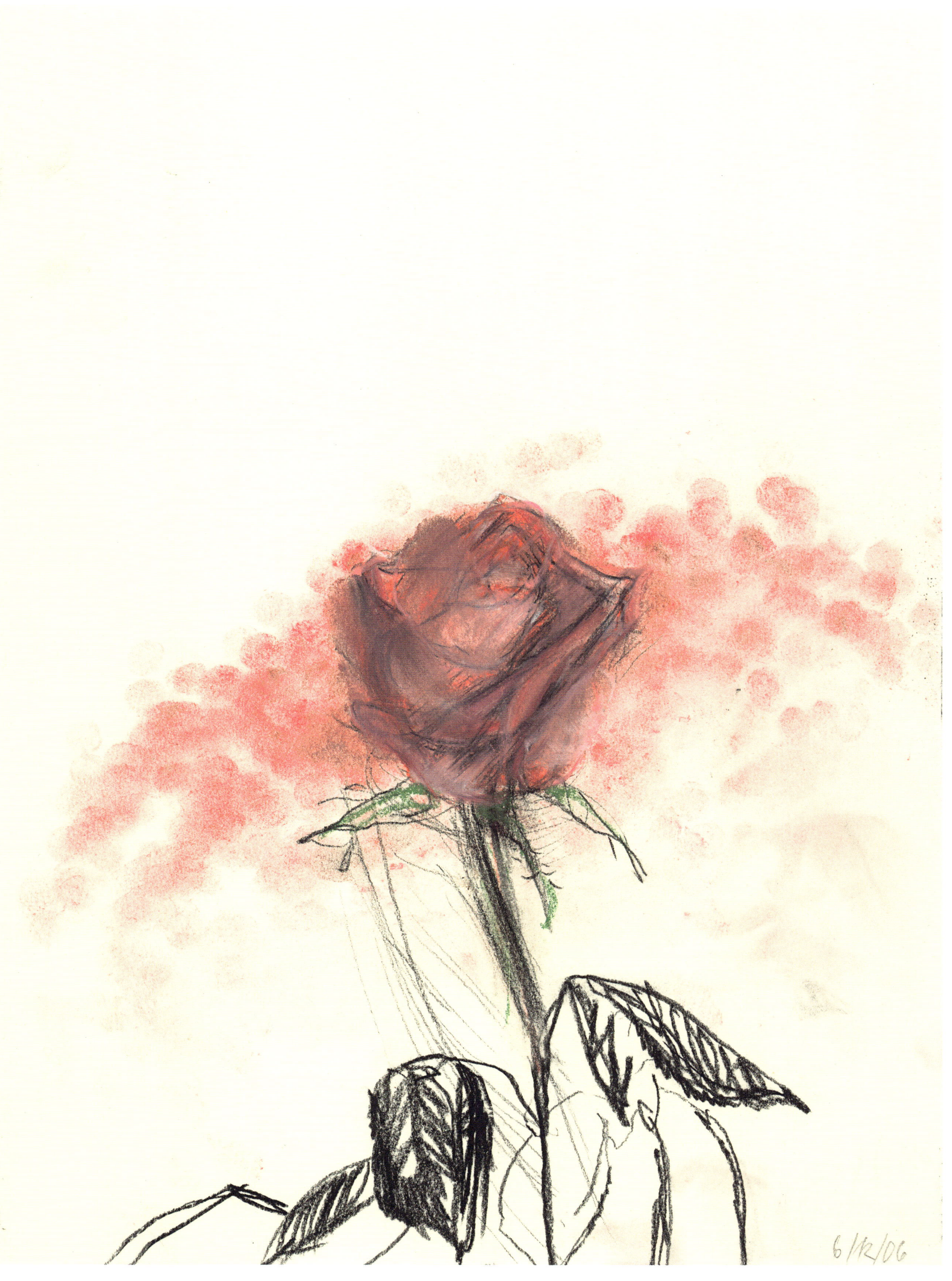
6/12/06

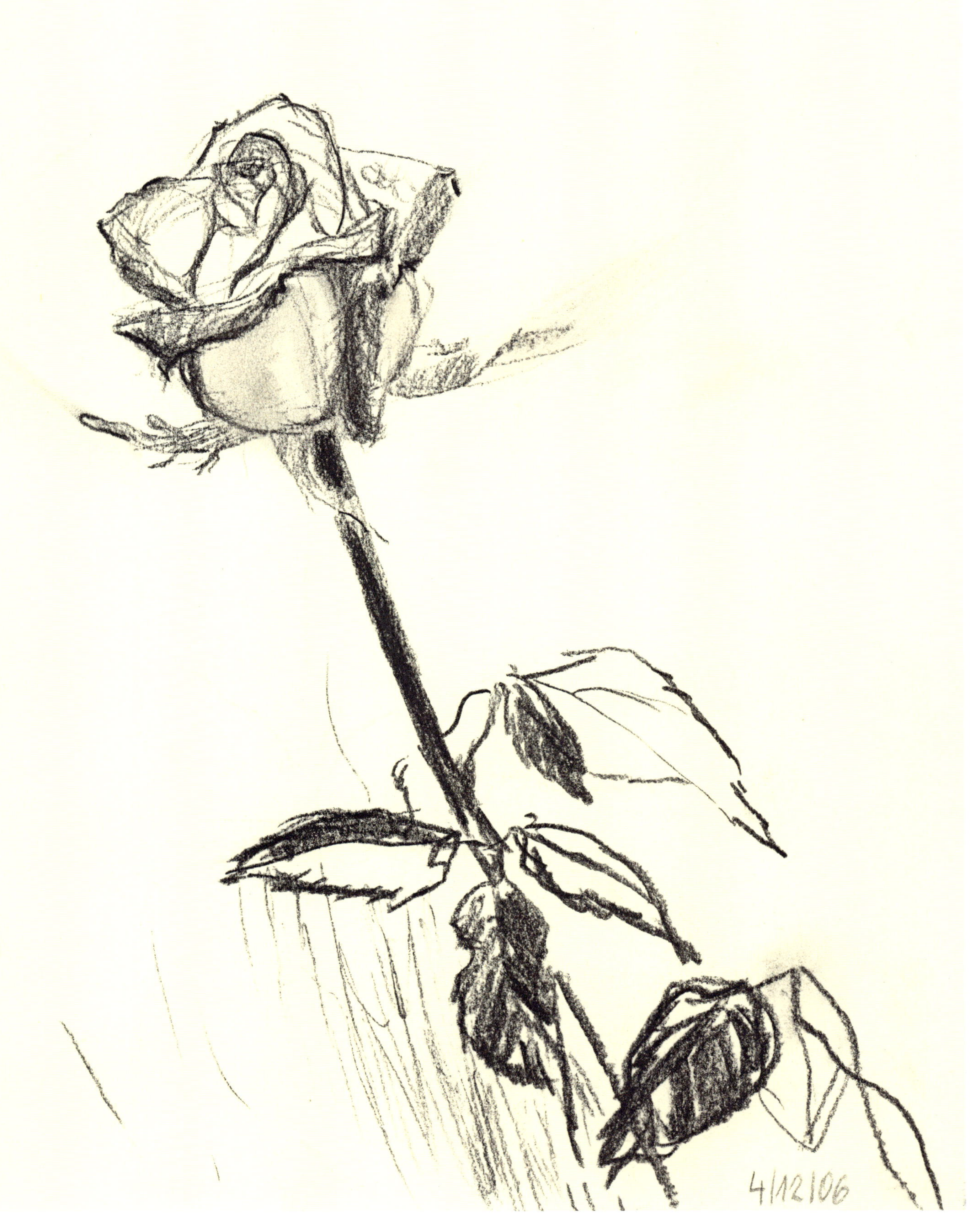
4/12/06

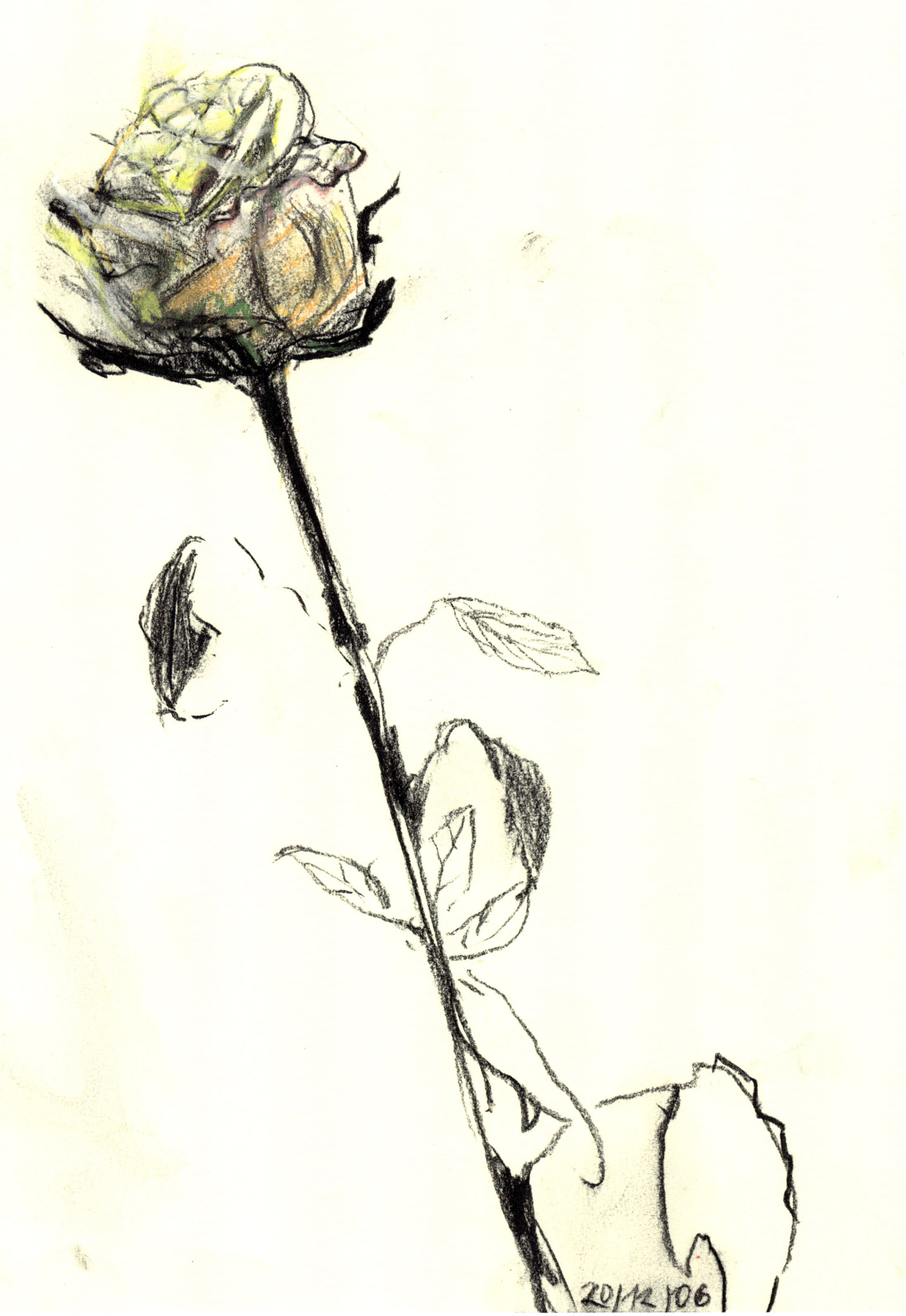

20/12/06

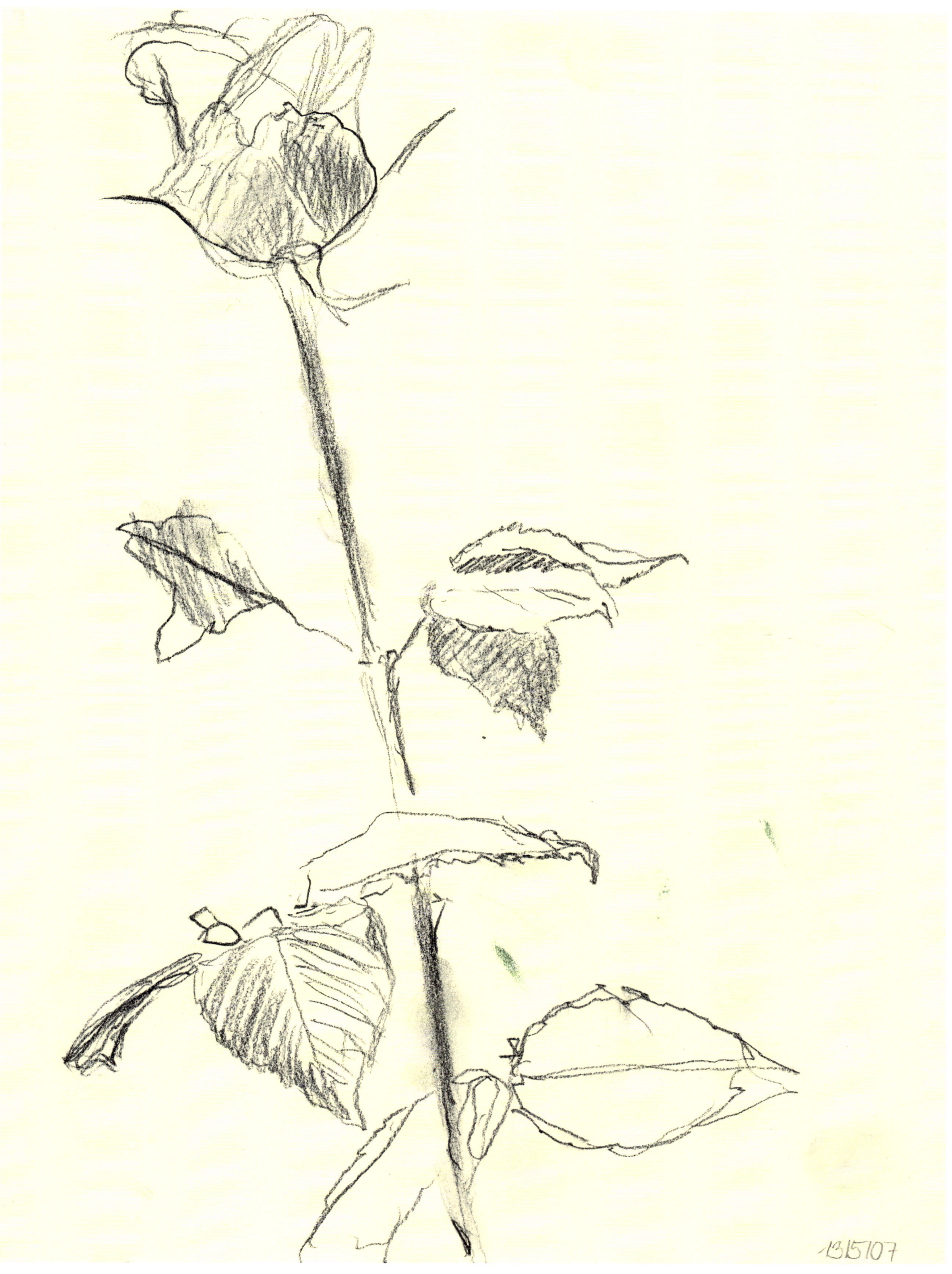
1315107

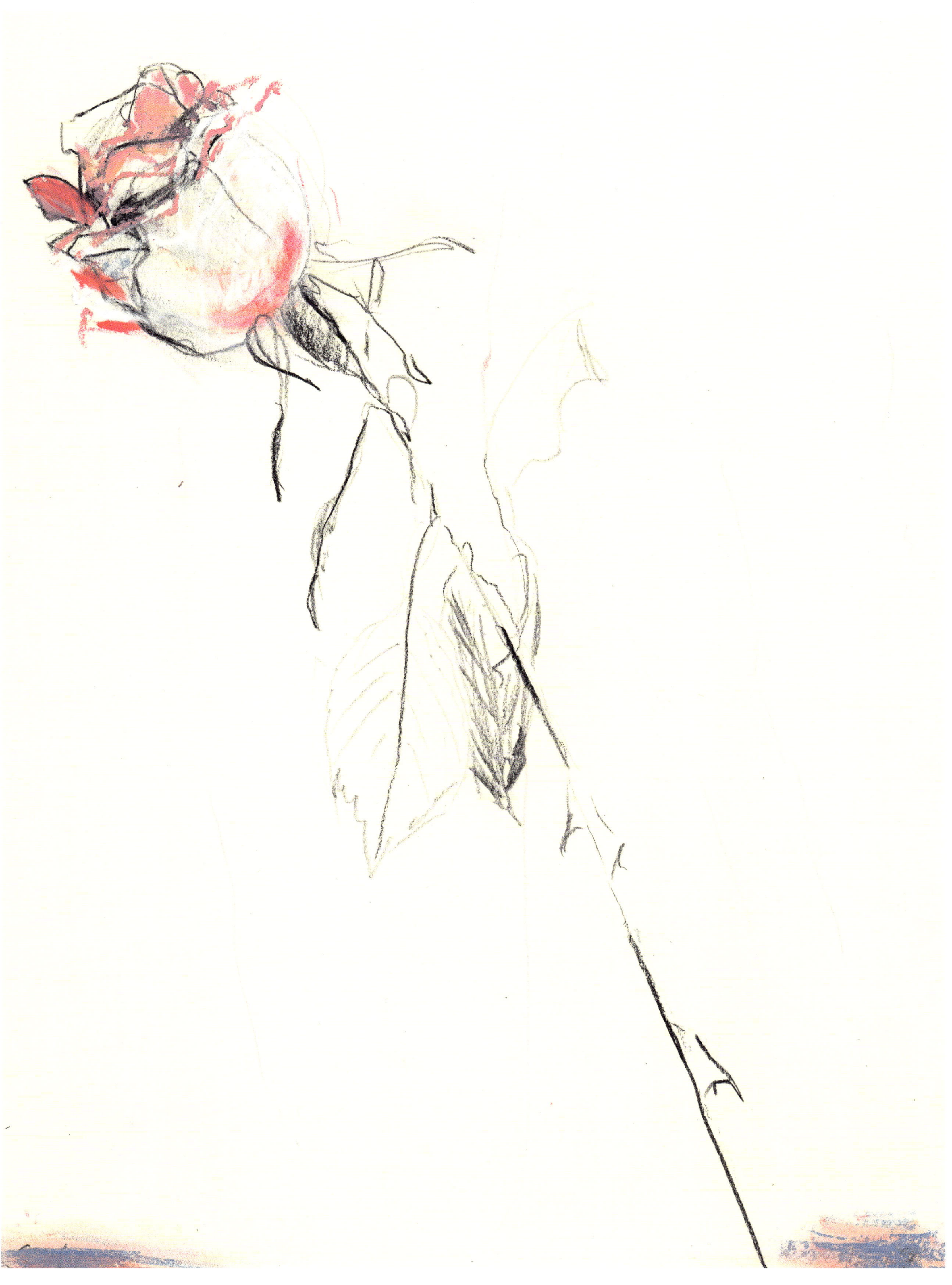

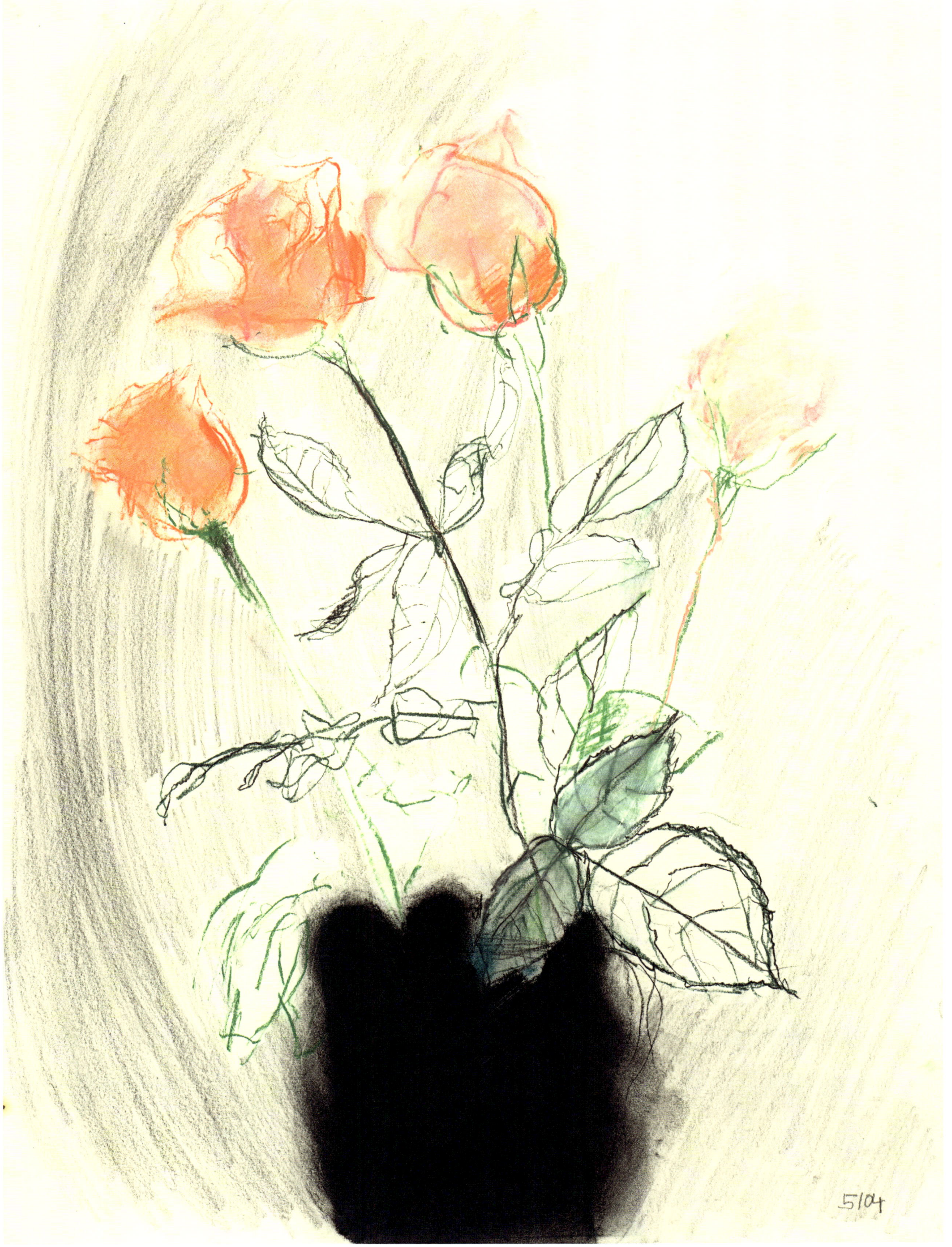

5104

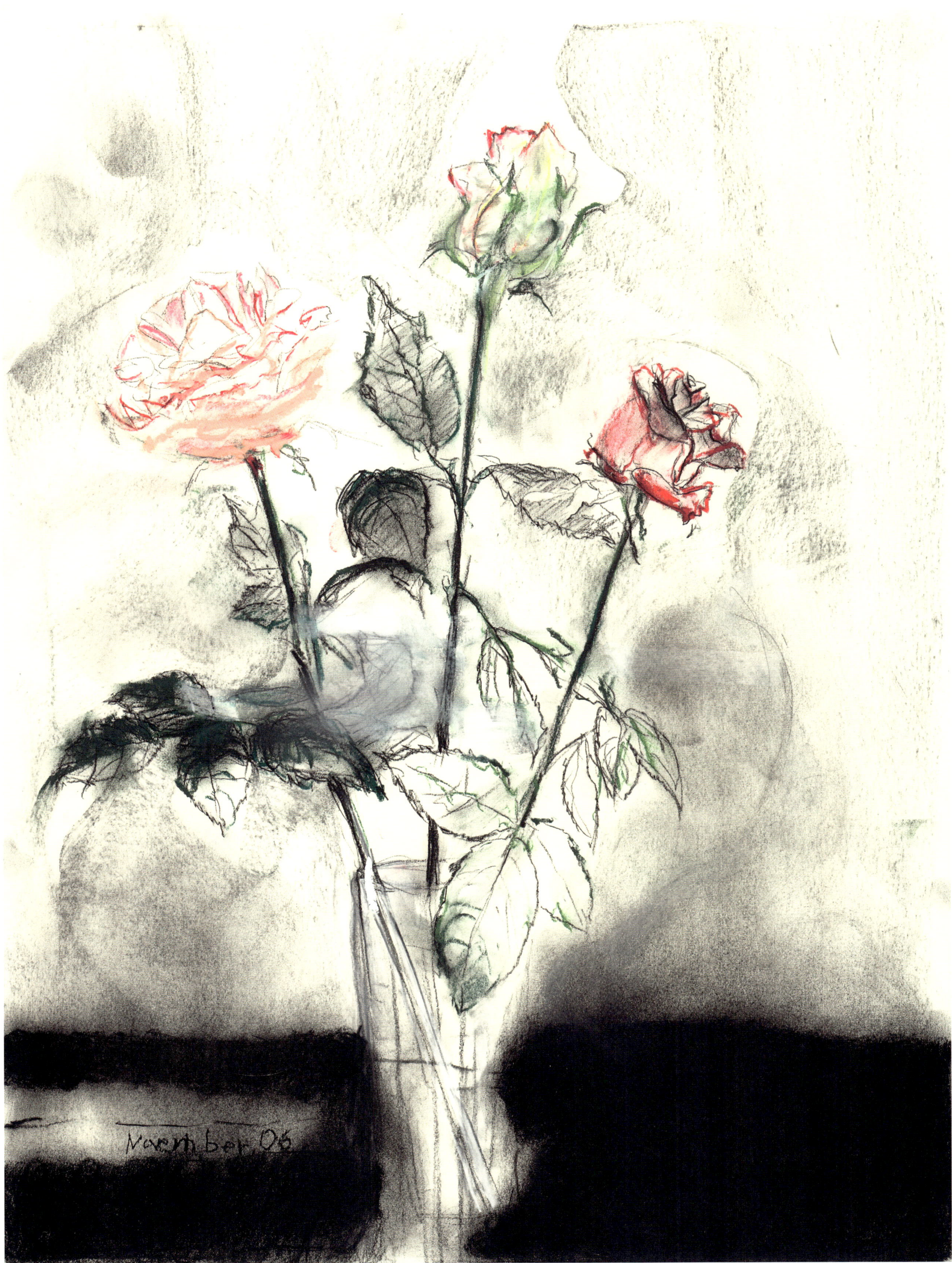

November 06

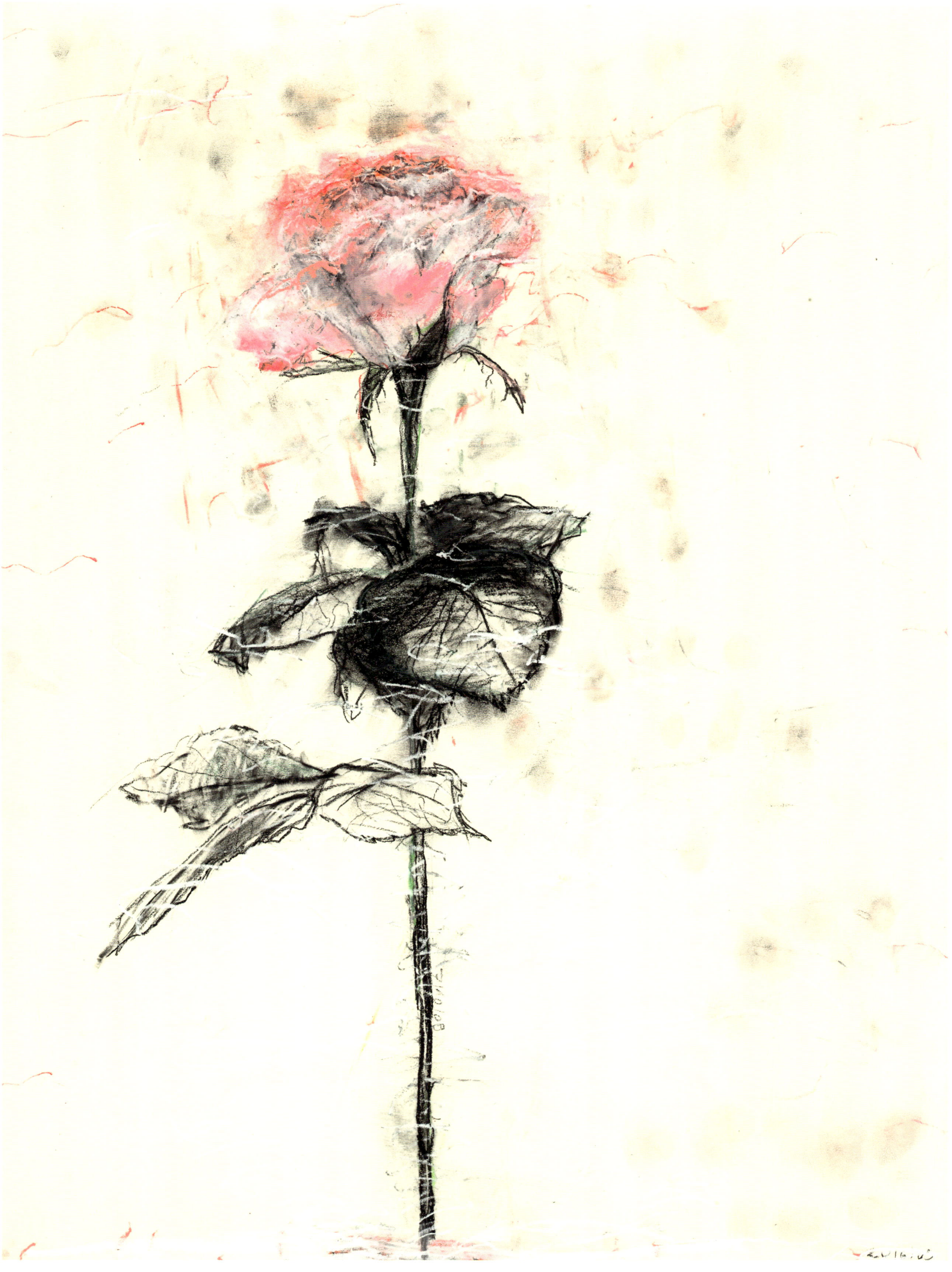

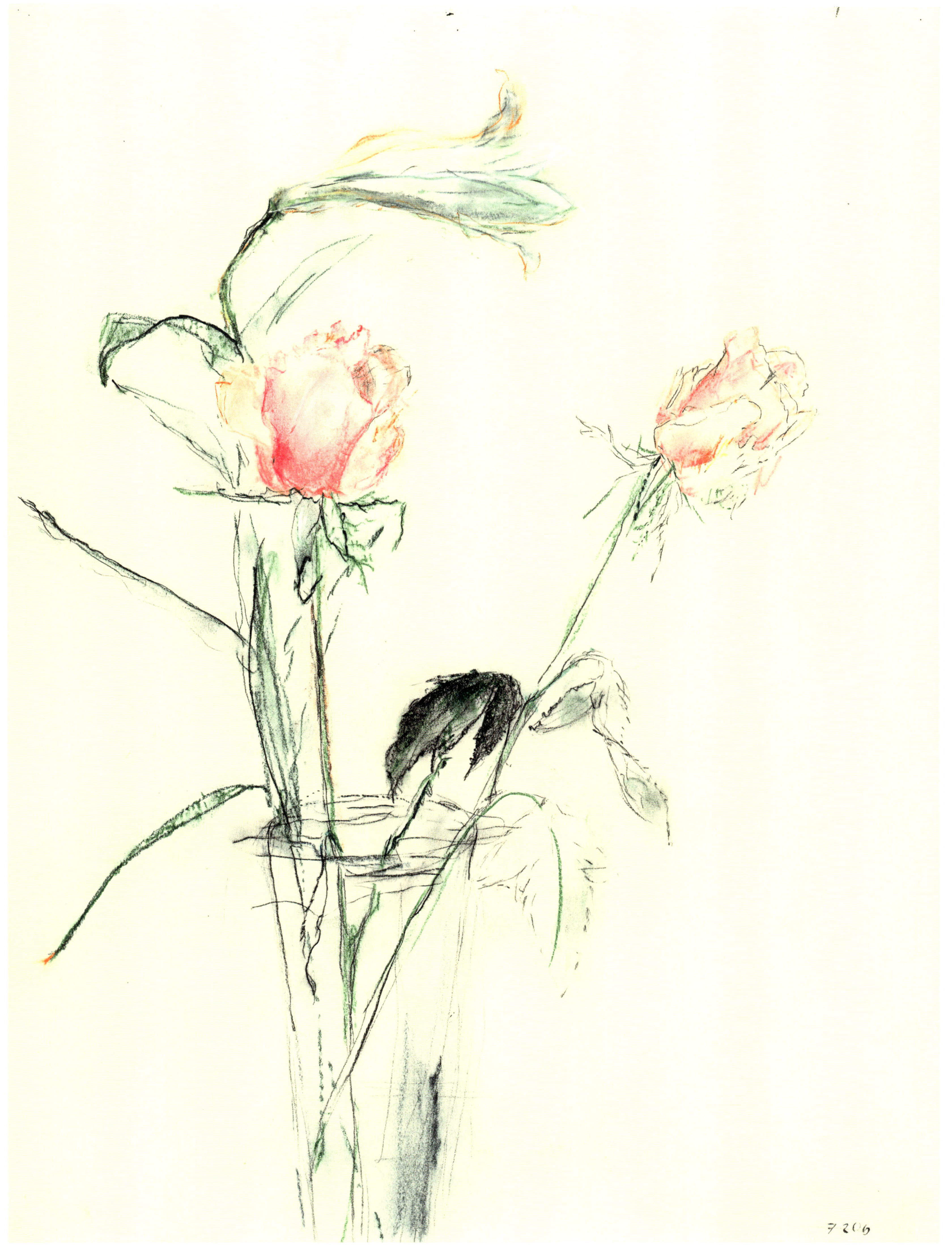

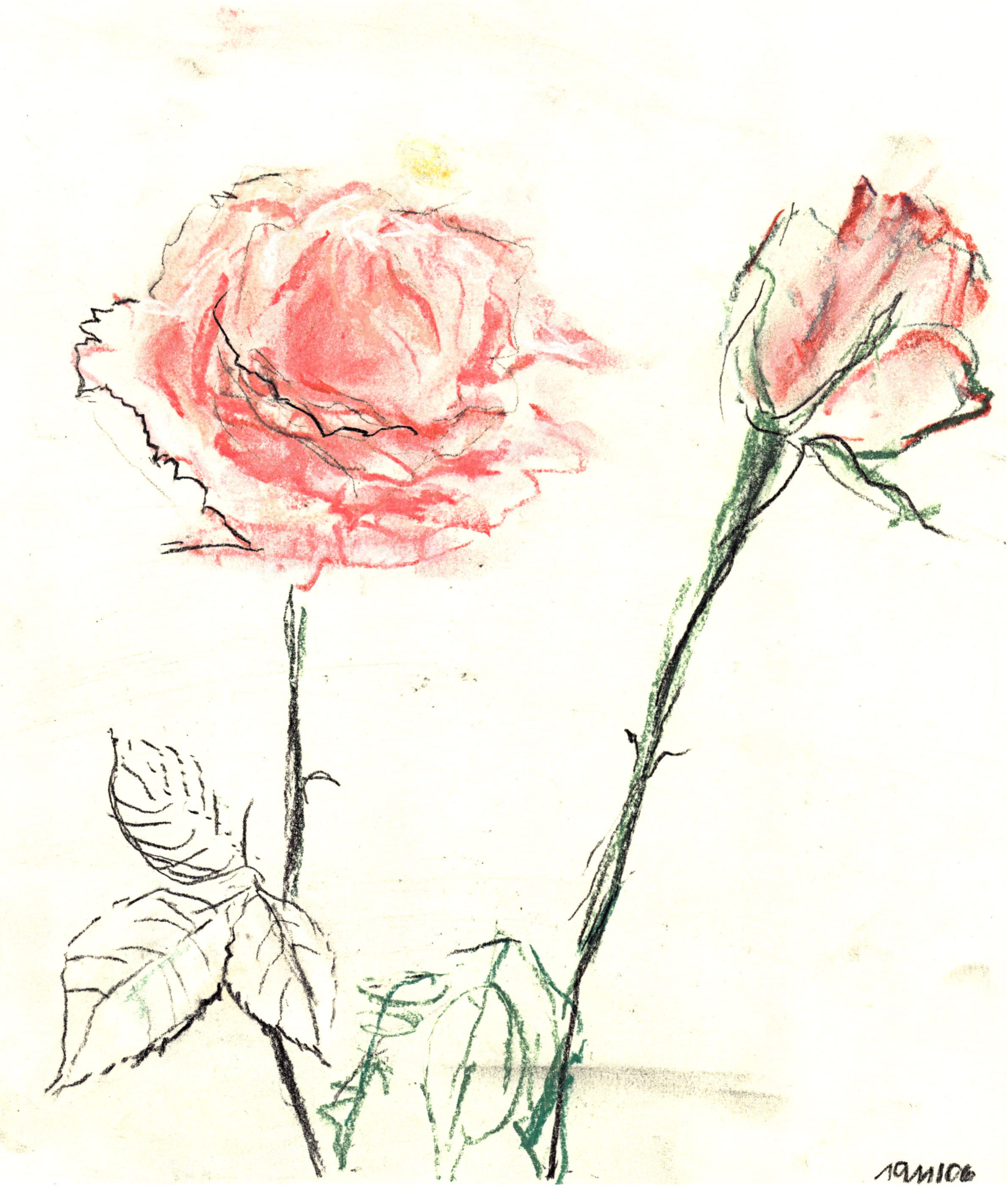
19/1/06

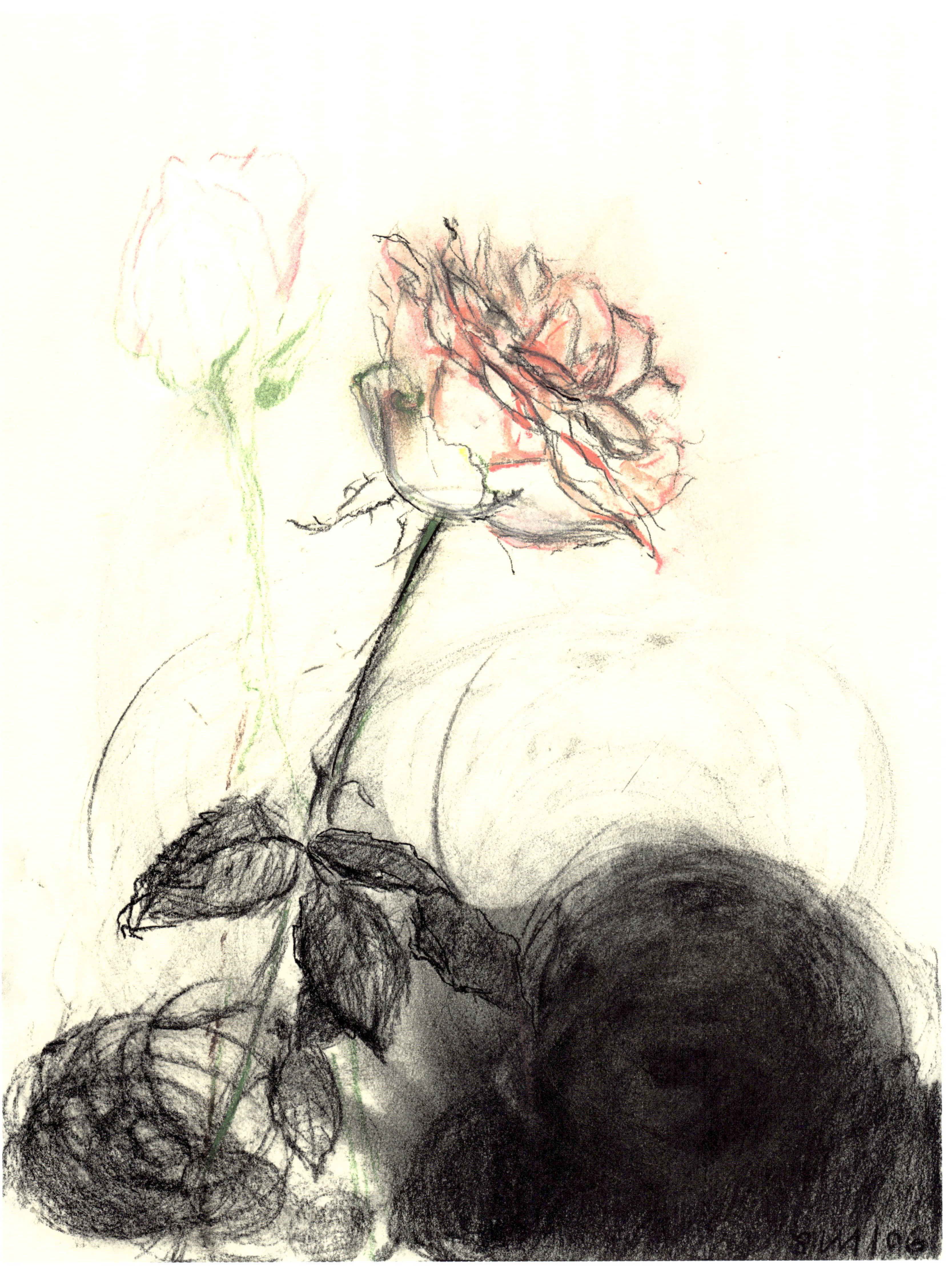

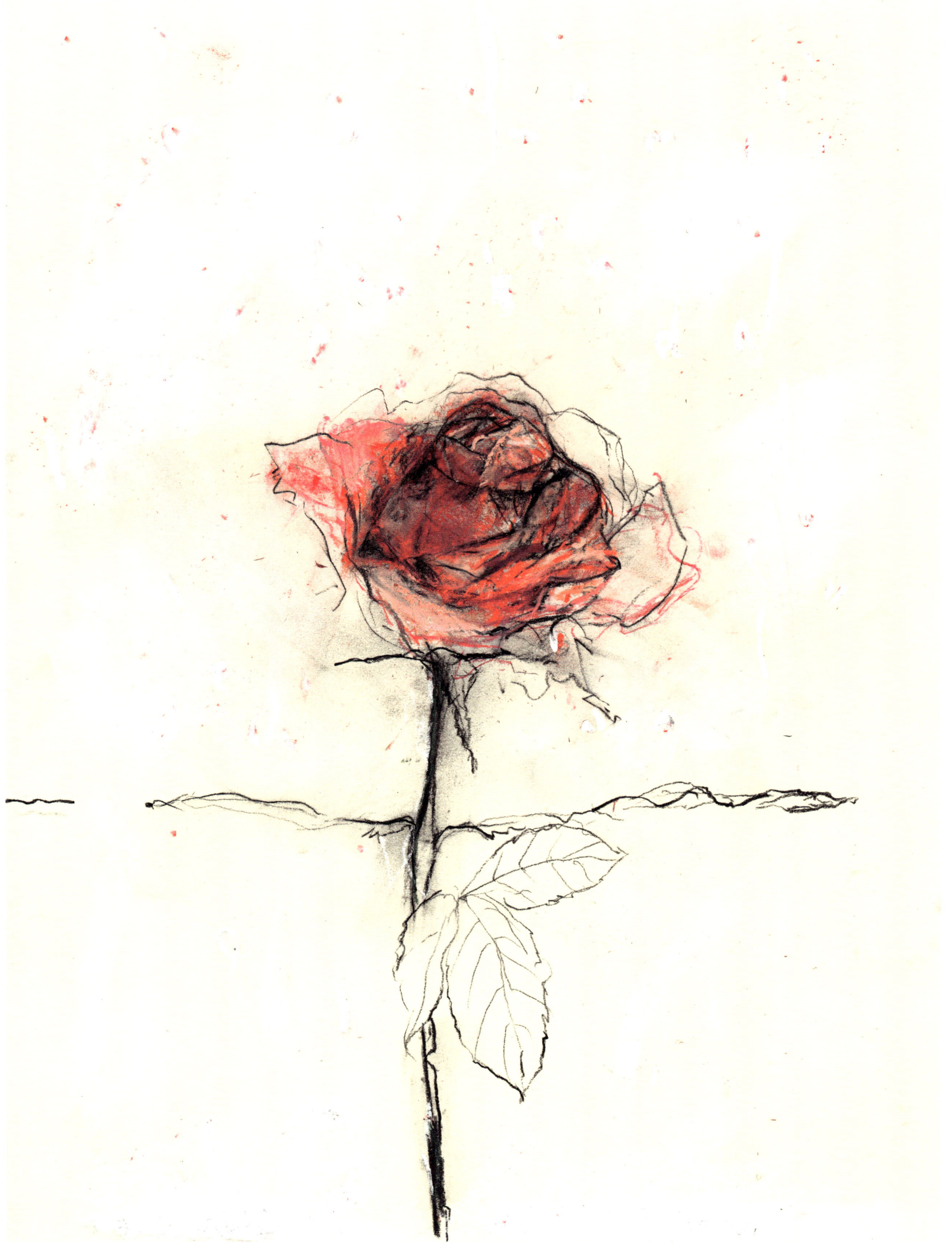

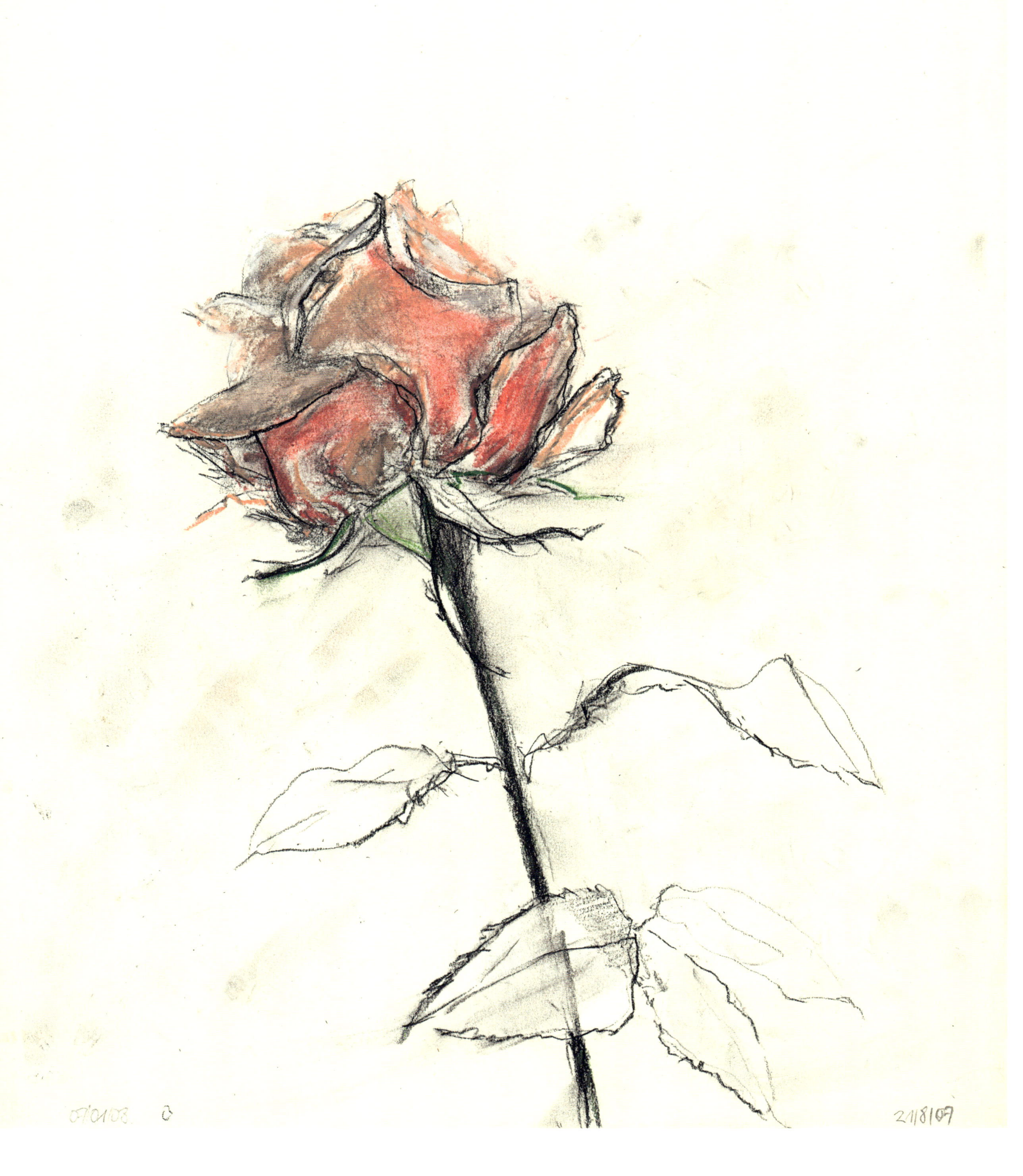
2/18/07

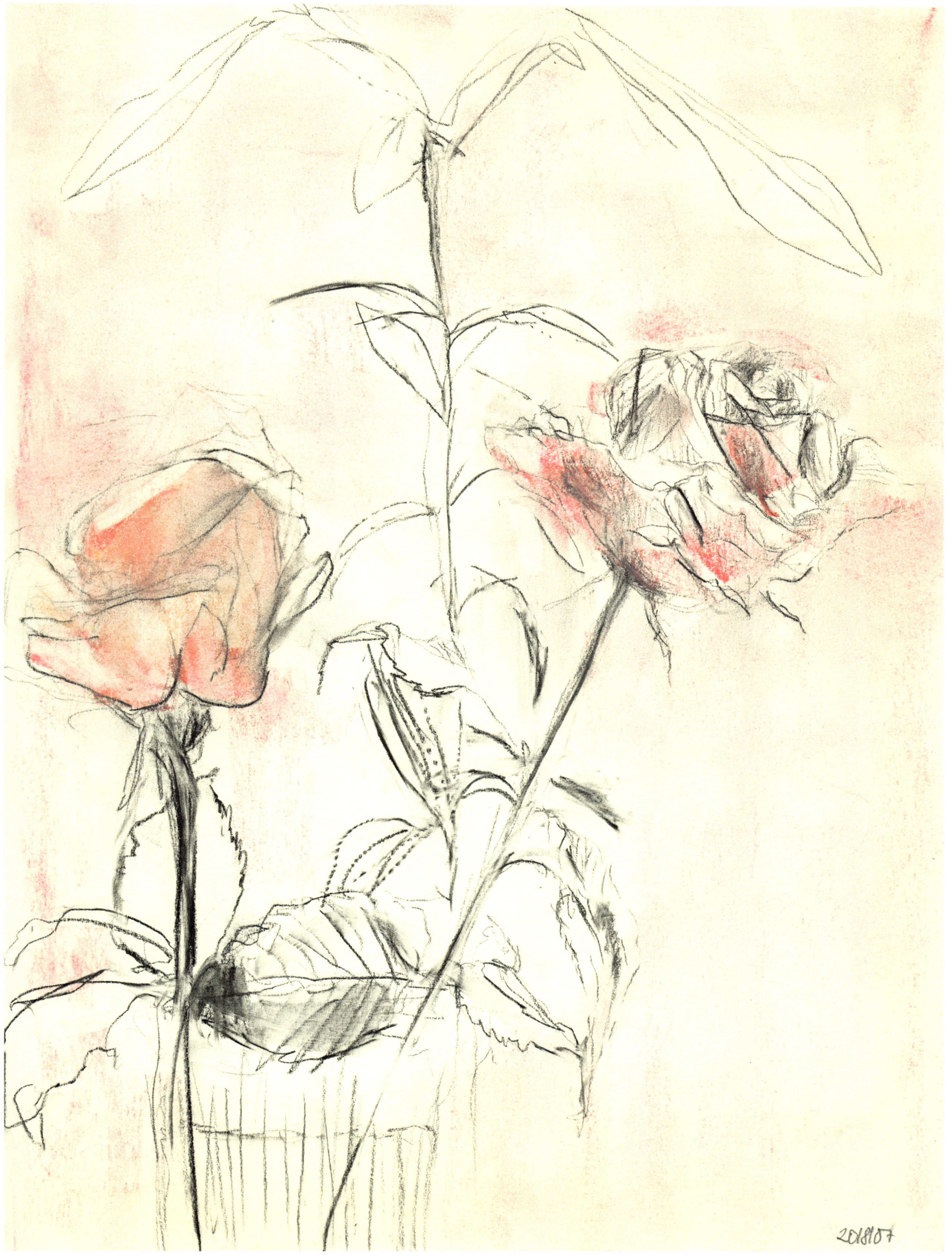

2018 07

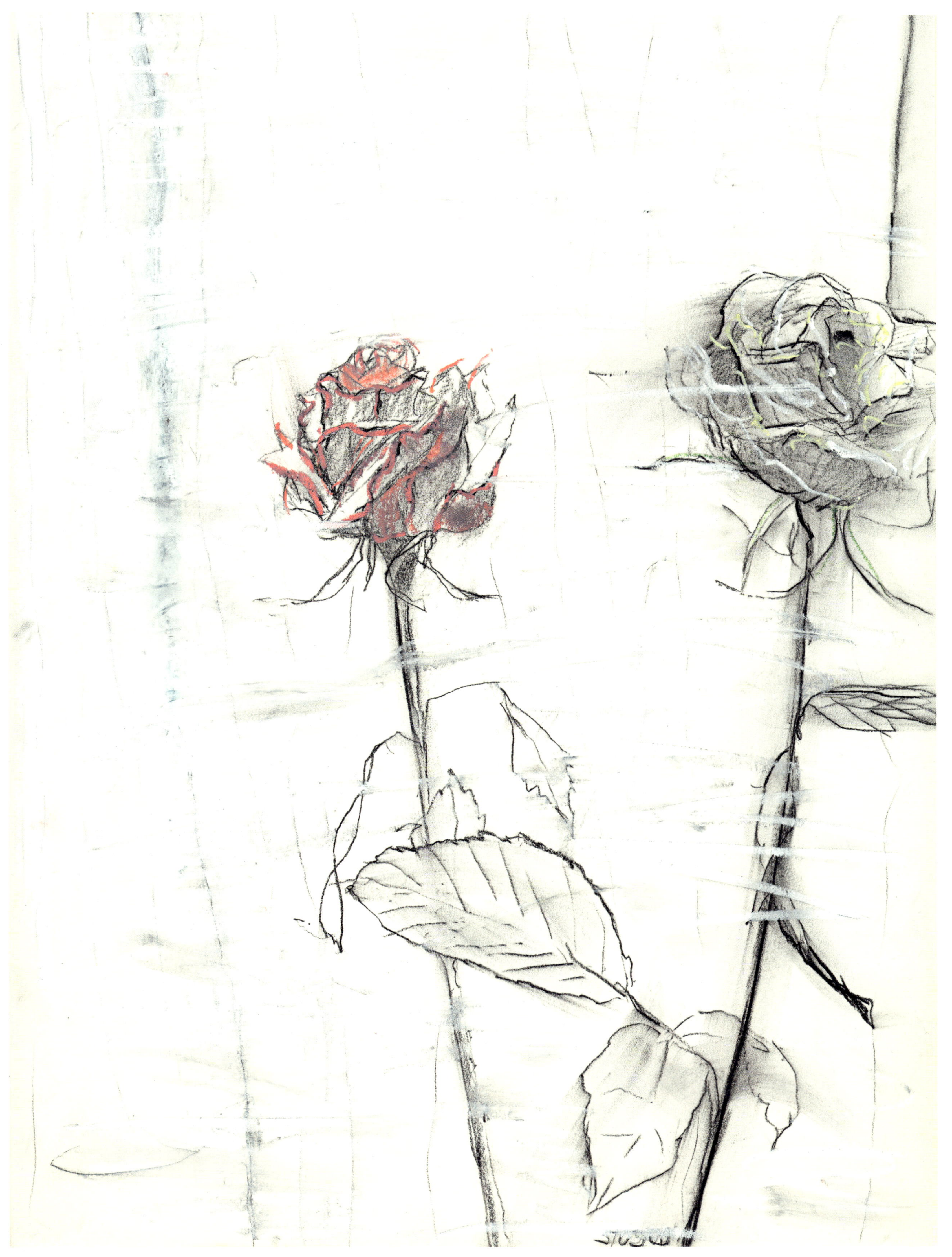

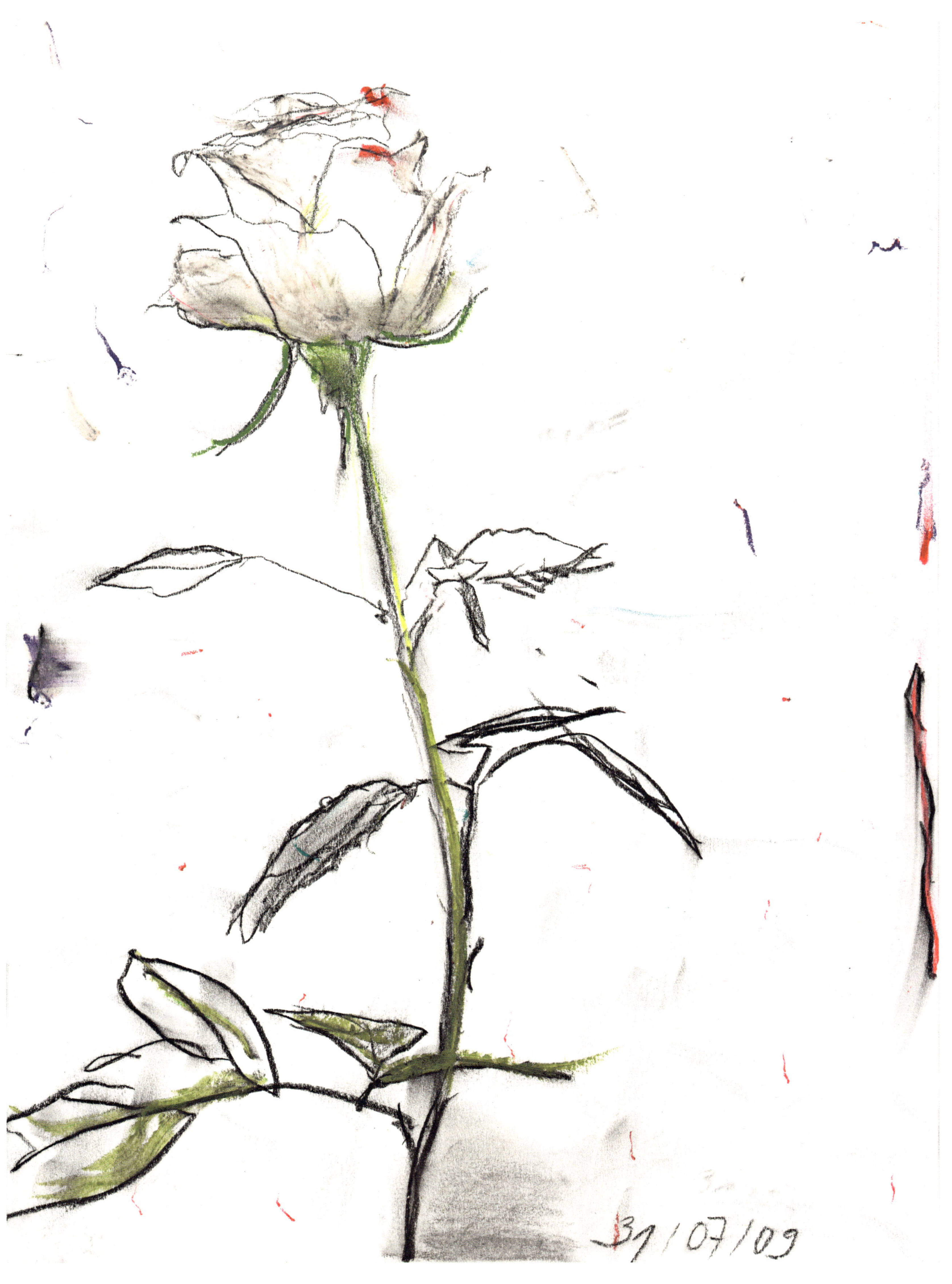
31/07/09

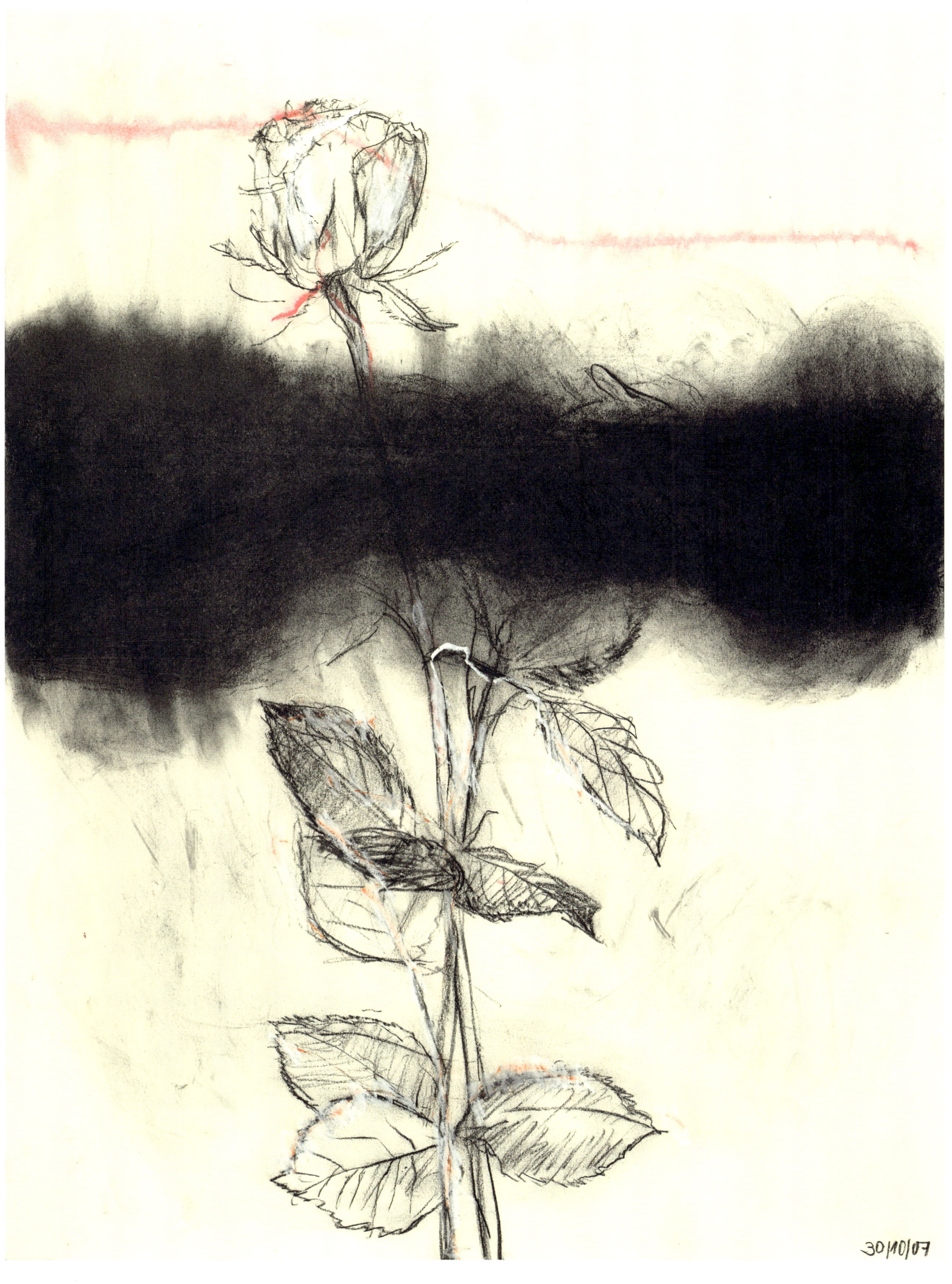

30/10/07

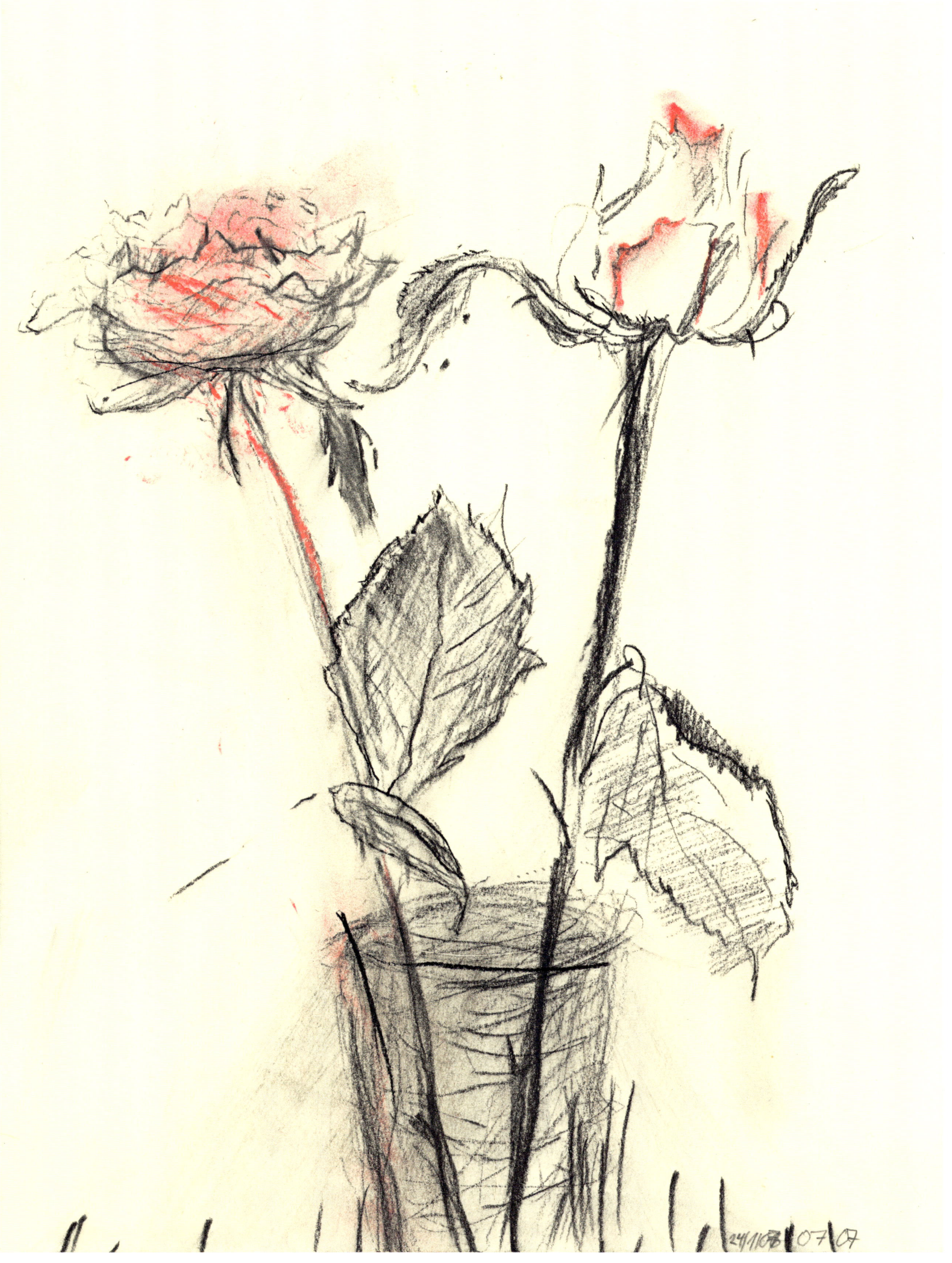

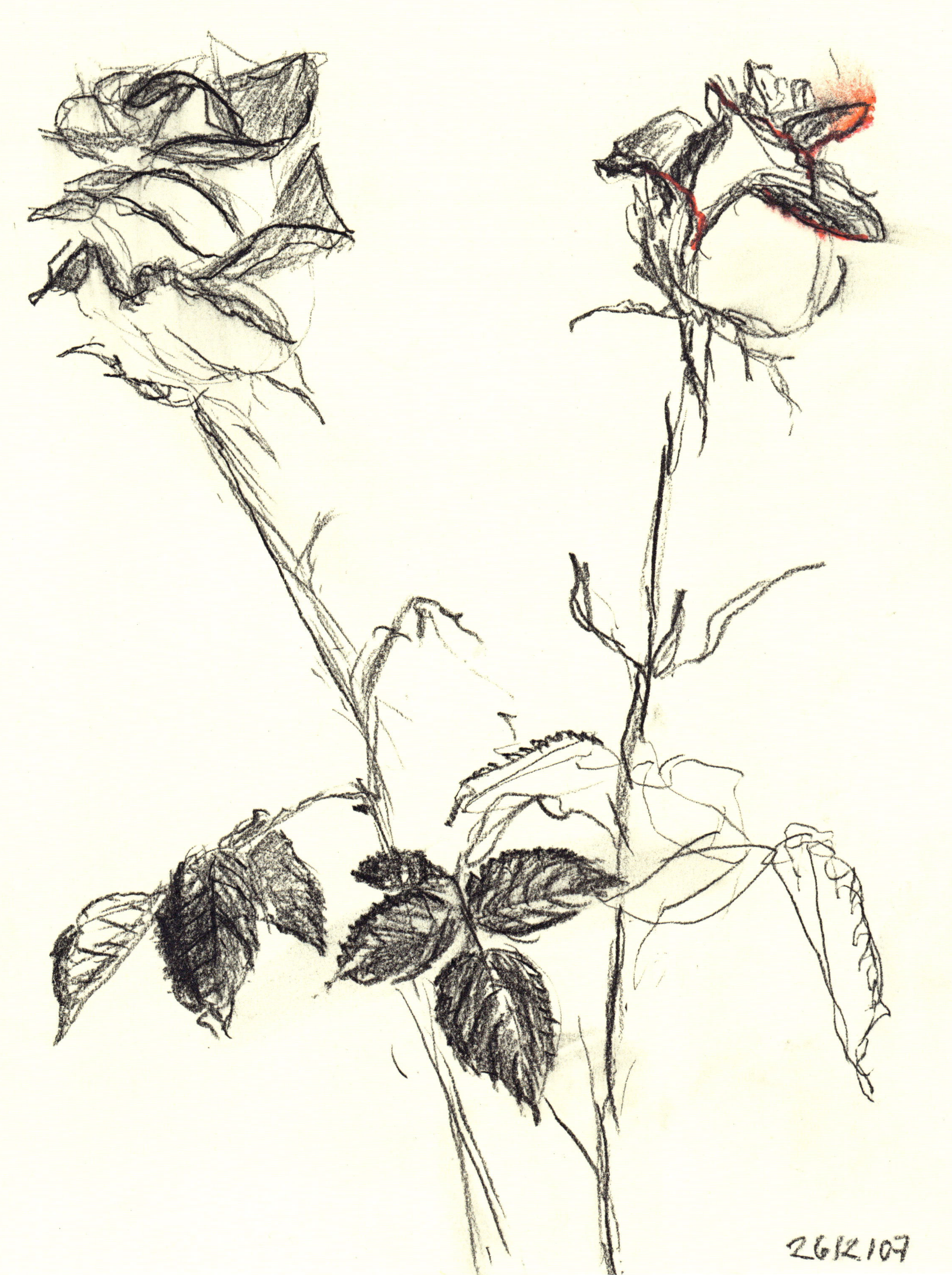

26.12.107

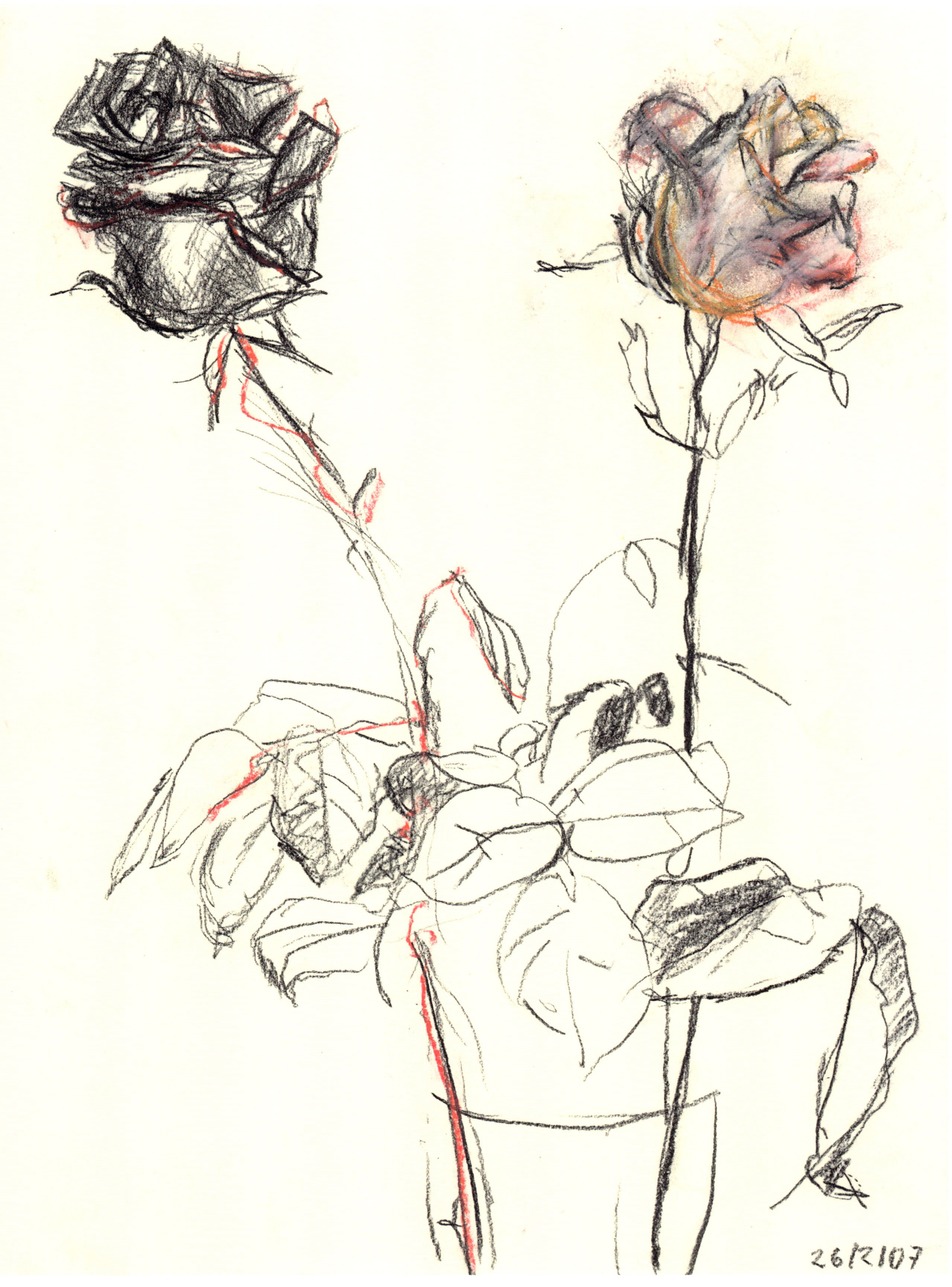

26/2107

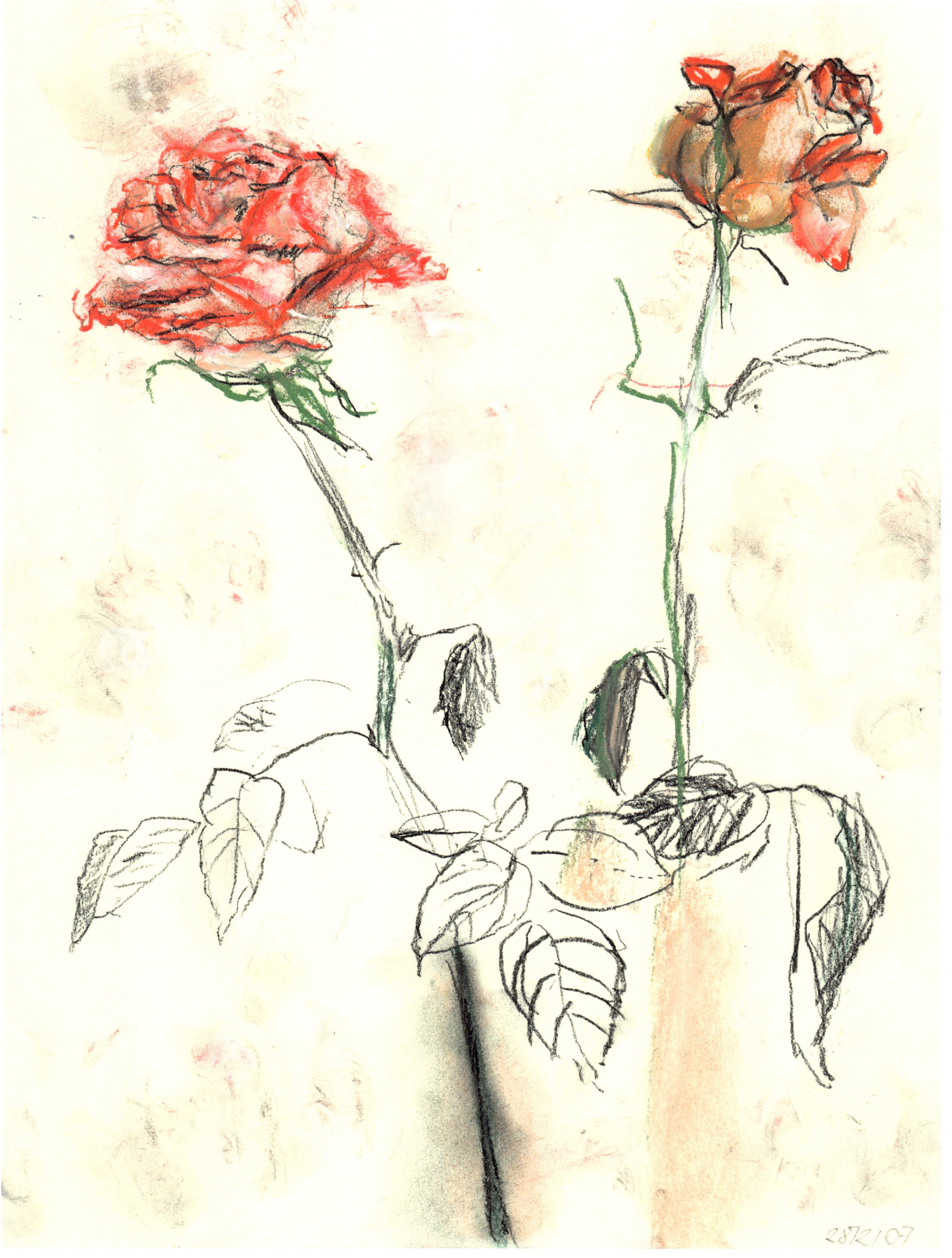
28/2/07

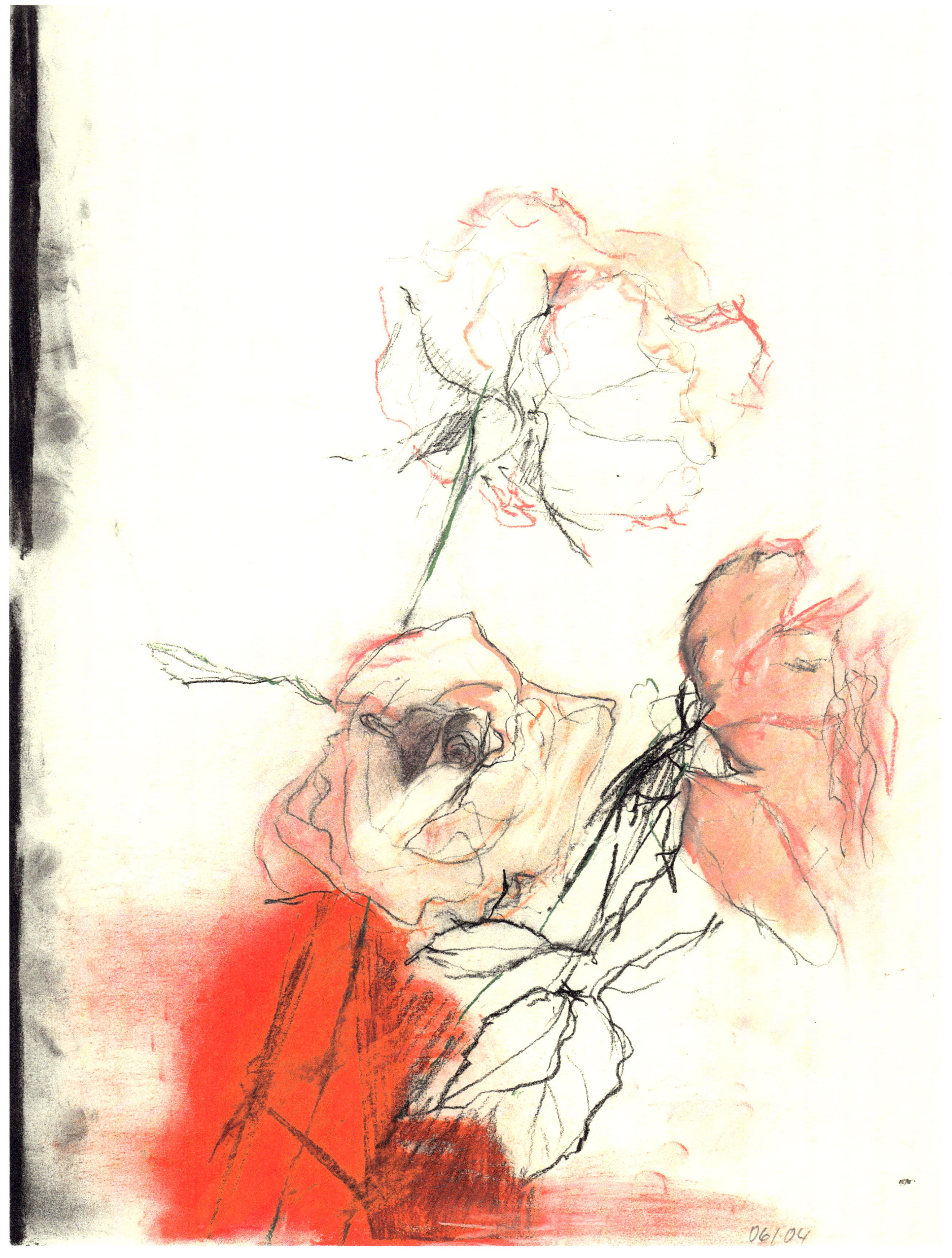
061·04

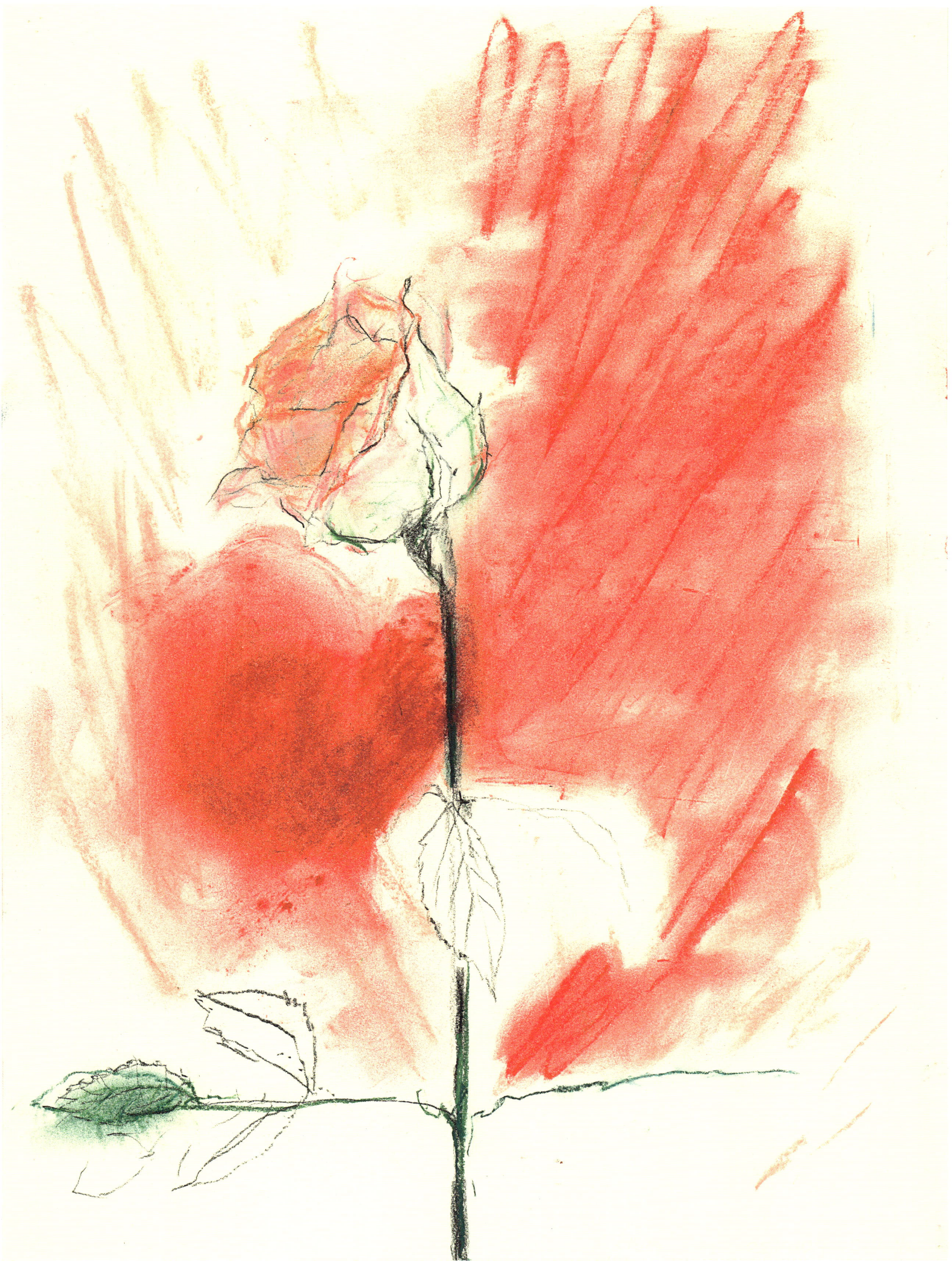

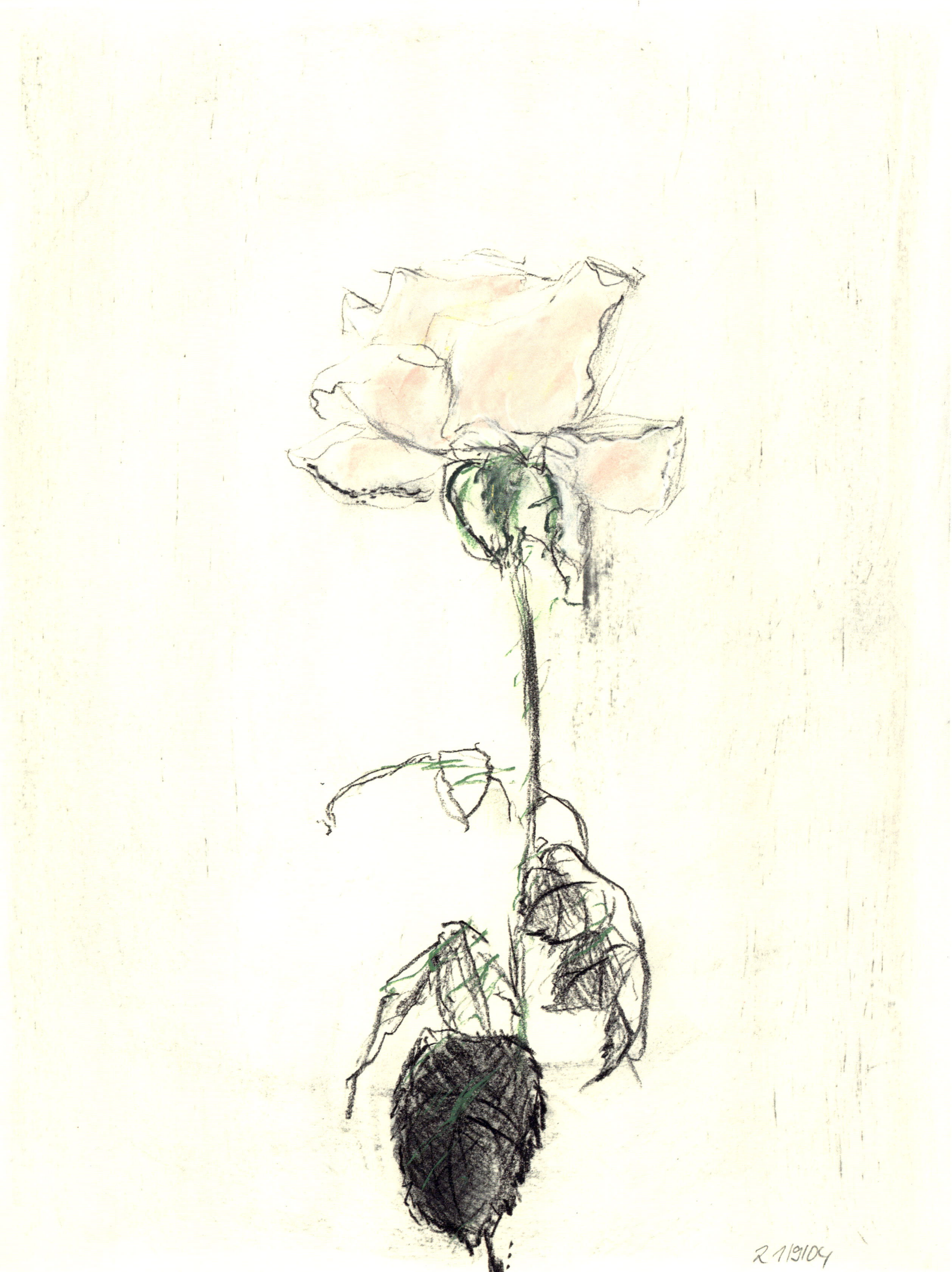
R 1|9|04

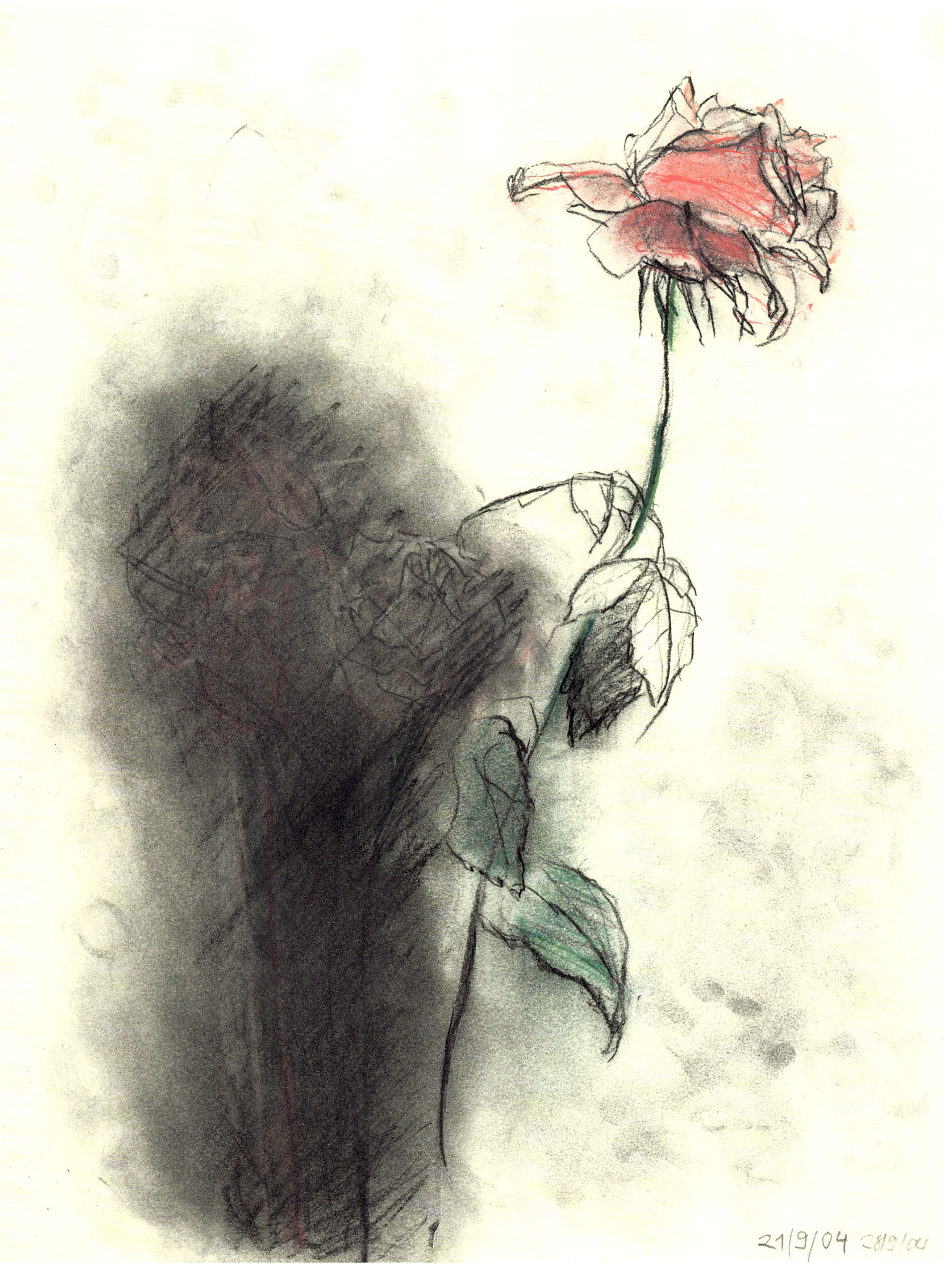

21/9/04

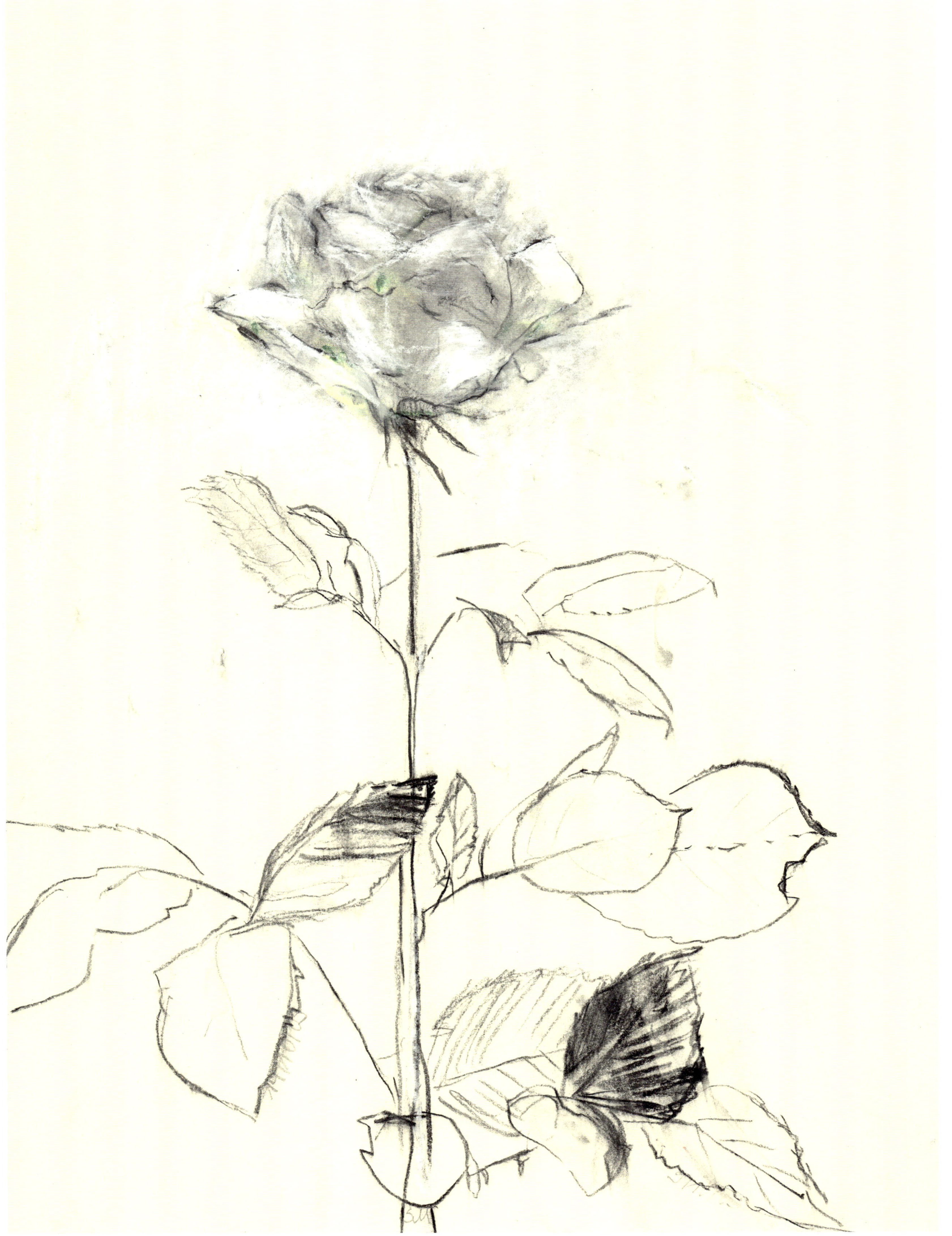

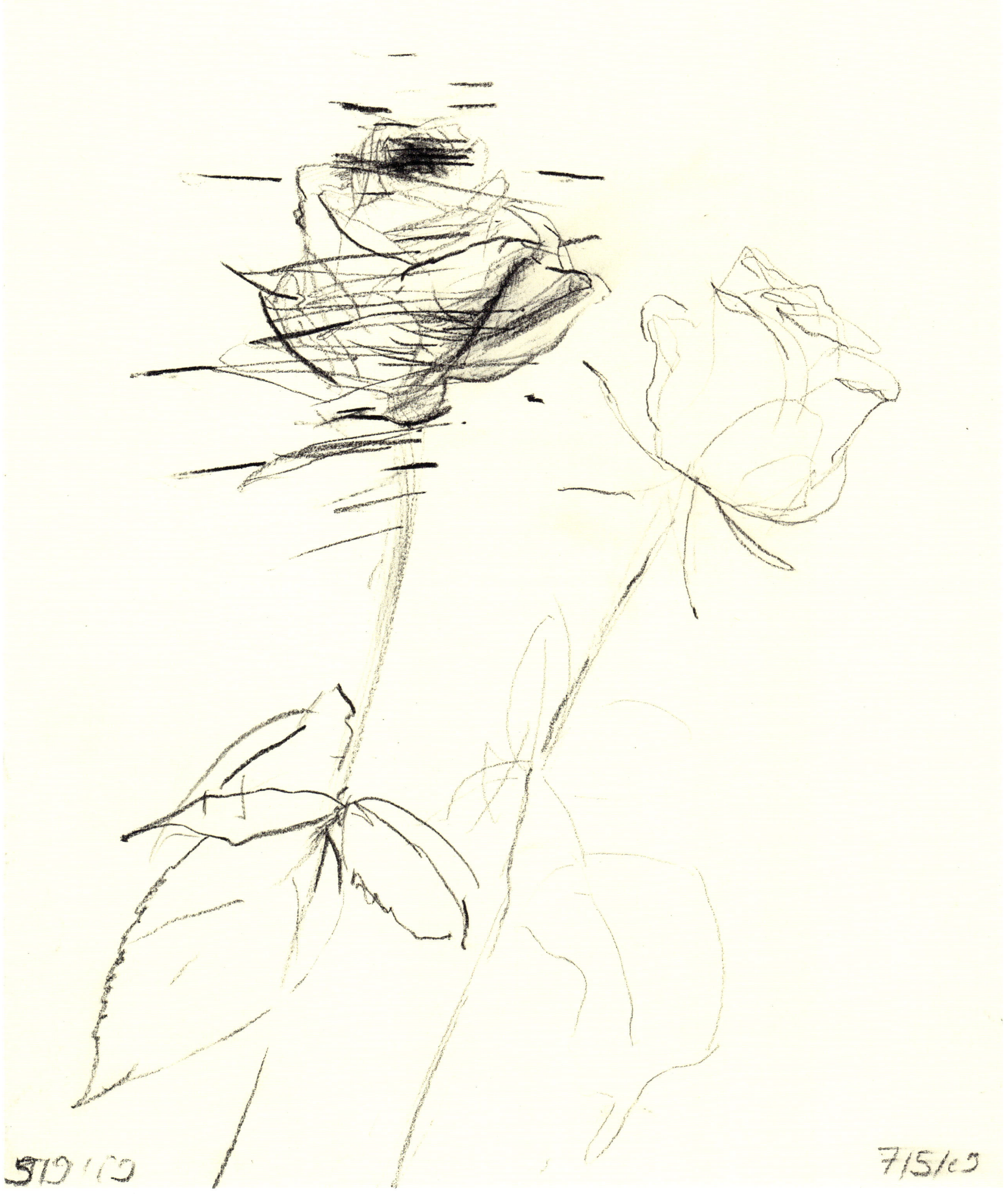

5/19/03
7/15/03

O rose, thou art sick!
The invisible worm
That flies in the night,
In the howling storm,

Has found out thy bed
Of crimson joy,
And his dark secret love
Does thy life destroy

— William Blake, c.1789

All drawings were created between 2004
and 2009. Their dimensions are 32 × 24 cm,
40 × 30 cm or 56 × 42 cm. The media are
charcoal, pastel or oil pastel on paper.

Poem (*The Green Windbreaker*): © 2009 Adam Zagajewski
(translated from the Polish by Clare Cavanagh)

Typesetting in Futura by Silke Fahnert, Uwe Koch, Cologne
Production by Printmanagement Plitt, Oberhausen

ISBN 978-0-9564041-2-1   Printed in Germany